The Unbound Soul
A journey of Self Discovey.

THE UNBOUND SOUL

First edition. October 4, 2024.

ISBN: 979-8227851789

Written by Seraphina Smith.

Dedication

To all the women who have dared to break free from the chains of societal expectations, who have dared to explore their deepest desires, and who have dared to embrace their authentic selves. This story is for you. May it ignite your journey of self-discovery and empower you to live a life that is truly your own.

Preface

I often find myself reflecting on the stories we tell ourselves and the stories we are told. As women, we are bombarded with messages about who we should be, how we should behave, and what our lives should look like. These messages can be subtle or blatant, whispered by society, our families, and even our own internalized beliefs. They can feel like an invisible cage, confining us to a predetermined path and shaping our identities.

This book is an exploration of the power of breaking free from these constraints, of reclaiming our narrative, and of embracing the fullness of our beings. It is a story about the woman we can become when we dare to question the narratives imposed upon us, when we dare to explore our darkest desires, and when we dare to choose a life that is authentically our own.

I believe that every woman has the power to unlock her unbound soul, to shed the limitations of societal expectations, and to embrace her true self. This story is a testament to that belief, and my hope is that it will resonate with you on a deeply personal level, inspiring you to embark on your own journey of self-discovery and liberation.

Introduction

Amelia stood before the mirror, her reflection staring back at her with a strange sense of familiarity, and yet, a growing feeling of unease. She had meticulously curated her life for years, presenting a perfect facade to the world. The "good girl" persona she had cultivated was flawless: a pillar of the community, a devoted daughter, a model student, a successful professional.

But behind the carefully crafted image, a different story unfolded. A story of unspoken desires, stifled dreams, and a yearning for something more. A longing for self-expression, for liberation, and for the freedom to explore the depths of her being.

As Amelia approaches her 30s, the cracks in her carefully constructed world begin to show. The "good girl" facade feels increasingly constricting, and a powerful voice whispers within, urging her to break free. Driven by a potent mix of fear and curiosity, she embarks on a journey of self-discovery, exploring the forbidden realms of her own desires, confronting the internal conflict between the "good girl" she has presented to the world and the "bad girl" she has suppressed.

This is Amelia's story, a journey of transformation, liberation, and self-discovery. It is a story of confronting the limitations of societal expectations, of embracing the complexities of womanhood, and of finding the courage to claim her own narrative.

Prepare to witness the unraveling of a life meticulously crafted and the emergence of a woman ready to reclaim her authentic self. This is a story about the power of vulnerability, the beauty of imperfection, and the enduring strength of the human spirit. It is a story about the unbound soul.

The Good Girl Persona

Amelia, at thirty, was a picture of perfection. Her life was a carefully curated tapestry woven with threads of societal approval and religious piety. She was the daughter of a devout Baptist family, her upbringing steeped in the rigid doctrines of a conservative faith. The world she knew was one where virtue was measured by adherence to a strict moral code, where "goodness" was synonymous with obedience and conformity.

Every fiber of her being had been trained to embody this "good girl" persona. She was the epitome of propriety, her every action measured and controlled. Her clothes were modest, her language clean, her relationships carefully vetted. She was a model citizen, a pillar of the community, a testament to the success of her upbringing.

Her world was a carefully constructed cage of expectations, and she was a prisoner within its walls. She had learned to navigate its confines with a practiced grace, suppressing her own desires and aspirations to fulfill the roles prescribed to her. She was the dutiful daughter, the devoted wife, the exemplary mother. She was everything she was supposed to be, yet deep down, a gnawing emptiness festered within her.

Amelia's days were an unending cycle of prescribed duties and obligations. She woke before dawn, the first rays of sunlight painting her room with a pale, ethereal glow. The scent of freshly brewed coffee mingled with the aroma of her mother's homemade bread, a comforting ritual that had been repeated for as long as she could remember. She joined her family for breakfast, a somber and silent affair, where the unspoken rules of conduct were as sacred as the scriptures themselves.

As the day unfolded, Amelia navigated the intricate choreography of her life, each step meticulously planned and executed. She worked as a teacher at the local Christian school, a role that allowed her to instill the same values in her students that had been so diligently instilled in her. She was a beacon of righteousness, a living embodiment of the ideals she believed in.

But beneath the surface, a quiet rebellion simmered. There were moments, fleeting and furtive, when a voice whispered from the depths of her soul, a voice that dared to question the confines of her reality. A voice that spoke of desires she had buried deep, aspirations she had stifled, and longings she had deemed forbidden.

The voice was faint, almost imperceptible, yet it grew louder with each passing year, its insistent whispers turning into a clamorous chorus. Amelia's carefully constructed world, a world that had once provided her with a sense of security and belonging, now felt like a suffocating prison. The chains of her upbringing, the constraints of societal expectations, and the shackles of her own internalized beliefs were beginning to tighten their grip, threatening to crush her spirit.

Her marriage, a union that had once been the pinnacle of her aspirations, now felt like a gilded cage. She had married a man chosen for her, a man who shared her faith and her values, and a man who was everything her parents had envisioned for her. Their life together was a picture of domestic bliss, a testament to the success of their shared beliefs. Yet, behind closed doors, a simmering resentment began to build.

She found herself yearning for something more, something that eluded her grasp. She felt a pull towards a world she had only glimpsed through the cracks in her carefully curated reality, a world where passion burned bright, where desires were embraced, and where individuality reigned supreme.

These whispers, these yearnings, were a constant source of anxiety. Amelia's internal conflict raged on. On one side stood the "good girl" she had been trained to be, the embodiment of righteousness and virtue, the unwavering embodiment of her family's faith. On the other side lurked the "bad girl", a being she had suppressed, a part of herself she had deemed unacceptable.

The "bad girl" whispered of forbidden desires, of exploring the depths of her sensuality, of breaking free from the constraints of her upbringing. She yearned for a world where she could shed the shackles of expectations and embrace her true self.

Amelia lived in a constant state of tension, caught between the pull of her carefully constructed world and the allure of the unknown. She knew that she couldn't continue living this way, trapped within a cage of her own making. But the thought of breaking free filled her with a mixture of terror and excitement.

She was afraid of what she might find if she ventured beyond the confines of her comfortable reality. She was terrified of betraying the expectations of her family, of shattering the image of righteousness she had so carefully cultivated. But even more, she was afraid of what she might discover about herself. The good girl persona had served her well for so long. It had provided her with a sense of security, a sense of belonging. But now, she realized that it was also a cage, a prison that had confined her true self for far too long. She was ready to break free, to shed the chains of expectations and embrace the unknown.

The first crack appeared when Amelia stumbled upon a book in the local library. It was a worn paperback with a faded cover, its pages filled with stories of women who had defied societal expectations and embraced their own desires. The stories were both alluring and terrifying. They spoke of women who had dared to challenge the status quo, to break free from the confines of their prescribed roles, to explore the depths of their own sexuality.

These stories resonated deep within Amelia, awakening a sense of longing she had long suppressed. She felt a surge of curiosity, a yearning to explore the parts of herself she had buried deep. She was afraid, but she was also exhilarated. She realized that there was more to life than the rigid framework she had always known. There was a whole world out there waiting to be explored, and she was finally ready to take a step into the unknown.

Amelia's journey to self-discovery was about to begin. She was about to embark on a transformative journey that would challenge her beliefs, test her limits, and ultimately lead her to embrace the freedom to be her true self. She was about to break free from the cage of expectations, to shed the shackles of her upbringing, and to embrace the unknown. She was about to become the "bad girl" she had always suppressed, and in doing so, she would find a liberation she had never dreamed possible.

The Cracks Begin to Show

The cracks in Amelia's carefully constructed life began to appear subtly at first, like hairline fractures in a seemingly perfect facade. It started with a nagging sense of dissatisfaction that she couldn't quite place, a feeling of emptiness that permeated her carefully curated existence. It was a stark contrast to the picture she projected – the successful lawyer, the devoted daughter, the "good girl" everyone admired. But beneath the surface, a yearning for something more, something different, was stirring within her.

It began innocently enough. A chance encounter at a local bookstore sparked a curiosity within her, a flicker of rebellion against the strict boundaries she'd always adhered to. She stumbled upon a book with a provocative title, "The Unbound Woman," and found herself drawn to its promises of self-discovery and liberation. Its pages, filled with stories of women breaking free from societal expectations and embracing their desires, resonated deeply with a part of her that had long been suppressed.

The book became her secret companion, a forbidden fruit she savored in stolen moments. It was a stark contrast to the religious texts she'd been raised on, texts that emphasized obedience, conformity, and the importance of suppressing her desires. Yet, there was a growing awareness within her that the "good girl" persona she'd cultivated was not entirely authentic. It was a carefully crafted mask she wore to protect herself from judgment and to appease the expectations of her family and community.

The cracks grew wider with each passing day. A chance encounter with a free- spirited artist at a gallery opening, a conversation with a coworker who spoke openly about her sexuality, and even a seemingly innocuous scene in a movie sparked a wave of questions within her. They were questions she'd never dared to ask before, questions that whispered of a world beyond the confines of her carefully constructed reality.

She started to notice the subtle ways she'd been conforming, the ways she'd been silencing her own desires to fit in. She saw the way her mother's voice echoed in her head, reminding her of the importance of being "good," of never straying from the path of righteousness. But something had shifted within her. The whispers of rebellion grew louder, challenging her ingrained beliefs and pushing her to confront the limitations she'd accepted as her own.

Amelia found herself drawn to unconventional experiences, seeking out opportunities that felt daring and liberating. She started taking dance classes, a form of expression she'd always considered frivolous and unfitting for a woman of her stature. She even dared to attend a concert with her friend, a night of loud music and wild abandon that felt exhilarating yet terrifying. The experience was a jolt to her system, a reminder that she was capable of letting go and embracing a side of herself she'd kept hidden for so long.

The more she stepped outside of her comfort zone, the more the cracks in her facade widened. The "good girl" she'd presented to the world began to crumble, revealing the woman she had always been but had never allowed herself to be. It was a process that was both exhilarating and terrifying, a journey that led her into the unknown and challenged her to confront her deepest fears and desires.

A growing sense of excitement was within her, a spark of rebellion that ignited a burning desire for liberation. Yet, there was also a profound fear, a fear of the unknown, of the potential consequences of straying from the path she'd been taught to follow. The fear of judgment, of disappointing her family, and of shattering the carefully constructed image she'd presented to the world.

But the yearning for something more, for a life that was indeed her own, became an irresistible force. It was a force that whispered promises of liberation, self- expression, and a world where she could be her most authentic self, unburdened by the expectations of others.

It was a dangerous and exhilarating journey, one that promised to transform her life but also carried the risk of shattering everything she'd ever known. The cracks in her facade had become a portal, a gateway to a new world where she could finally shed the shackles of her past and embrace the wild, untamed woman within.

The First Glimpse of the Bad Girl

The scent of lavender soap and freshly baked bread clung to the air, a comforting reminder of the life I'd carefully curated. My tiny apartment, with its pastel walls and carefully arranged bookshelves, was a testament to the "good girl" persona I'd built over the years. A persona crafted from the expectations of my family, church, and the society I'd been raised in.

Yet, lately, an unsettling restlessness had begun to stir within me, a whisper of rebellion against the carefully constructed facade. It started with a fleeting thought during a sermon, a question about the rigid interpretations of faith that felt like shackles on my soul. Then came the unsettling realization that my carefully chosen career path, designed to appease my parents and fulfill societal expectations, felt like a hollow shell, devoid of any genuine passion.

This restlessness, this yearning for something more, started to manifest in the most unexpected ways. A flicker of fascination at a racy novel I stumbled upon in the library, the sudden urge to wear a dress that hinted at a rebellious spirit, a late-night browsing of websites that explored the fringes of sexuality, topics I'd been taught to avoid. These forbidden thoughts, these whispers of desire, were both terrifying and exhilarating.

One evening, a chance encounter with a woman named Luna at a local bookstore sent a jolt of electricity through my carefully constructed world. Luna, with her bright red hair, ripped jeans, and a look in her eyes that spoke of a life lived on her terms, was everything I wasn't. As she spoke with passion about her latest artistic endeavors, a world of possibilities opened up before me, a world where art wasn't confined to the confines of religious dogma but a vibrant expression of the soul.

That night, as I lay in bed, the image of Luna, her fearless spirit, and her unapologetic self-expression filled my thoughts. For the first time, I dared to imagine a life outside the strictures of my carefully constructed reality, a life where I wasn't defined by societal expectations or religious pronouncements. The "bad girl," the one I'd always been told to suppress, emerged from the shadows, a mischievous whisper in the back of my mind.

The fear was undeniable, a cold knot in my stomach at the thought of stepping out of line, of defying the expectations that had shaped my entire life. Yet, alongside the fear, a powerful yearning for freedom, for self-expression, for a life truly my own, began to take root. The "bad girl" within me, so long silenced, was demanding to be heard.

The whispers turned into a chorus, a growing sense of urgency that resonated within me. The "good girl" persona, so carefully constructed, started to feel like a cage, a gilded prison I'd built for myself. The realization was both terrifying and liberating, a crack in the foundation of my carefully curated life that threatened to shatter the whole structure.

The question that now resonated within me was no longer "what will others think?" but rather, "what do *I* want?" The answer, though still unclear, whispered of a world beyond the boundaries of my comfort zone, a world where the "bad girl" might not be so bad after all. It was a world that held the promise of adventure, of self-discovery, and the exhilarating possibility of finally being true to myself.

The Fear of Letting Go

The Fear of Letting Go

The weight of the world felt like a physical entity pressing down on Amelia's chest, a constant reminder of the expectations she was supposed to live up to. She was the "good girl," the embodiment of everything her conservative upbringing had deemed acceptable. She went to church every Sunday, volunteered at the local soup kitchen, and had never even dared to think about questioning the strict moral code she had been taught. But lately, a nagging unease had been creeping into her carefully curated life.

It wasn't a sudden revelation, more like a series of tiny cracks that slowly spread across the facade of her perfect world. The first crack came when she saw a woman on the street, her clothes revealing more skin than Amelia had ever considered appropriate. A wave of curiosity washed over her, followed by a swift jolt of guilt. She quickly dismissed it as a fleeting thought, a momentary lapse in her carefully constructed reality.

But then came the second crack, a seemingly innocuous encounter at a coffee shop. She overheard a conversation between two women, their laughter light and carefree as they discussed a weekend getaway to a "secret beach" where they planned to "let loose." The words hung in the air, a siren song to a part of Amelia she didn't even know existed. A part of her, a forbidden and deeply hidden part, longed to break free from the constraints of her "good girl" persona and experience the wild freedom she witnessed in those two women.

The fear was a formidable foe, a constant whisper in the back of her mind reminding her of the consequences of deviating from the path she was supposed to follow. She saw the disapproving looks of her parents, heard the judgmental whispers of the church elders, and felt the weight of societal expectations crushing her spirit. What would her friends think? What would her community say? Could she truly live with the shame of betraying everything she had ever been taught?

The thought of letting go, of embracing the unknown, was terrifying. It felt like a leap into the abyss, a surrender to the darkest desires that lurked beneath the surface of her carefully cultivated persona. She knew that true freedom meant relinquishing control, allowing herself to be vulnerable, and opening herself up to the possibility of being judged, ostracized, even rejected. The fear of the unknown, of stepping outside the comfortable confines of her "good girl" cage, was almost paralyzing. But there was a flicker of something else within her, a tiny ember of defiance burning bright. It was a whisper of rebellion, a longing for something more, a yearning to break free from the shackles of expectations and discover the woman she was truly meant to be. The fear was still there, a heavy presence looming over her, but the ember of rebellion grew stronger with each passing day. It was a force that could not be ignored, a primal urge that whispered to her soul, "What if you could be more? What if you could live a life that is truly your own?"

This was the question that haunted Amelia's waking hours, the voice that refused to be silenced. She was trapped in a cage of expectations, a prisoner of her own carefully constructed persona, but the bars were beginning to rust, the walls were starting to crumble. The fear of letting go was real, but so was the longing for liberation, the desire to break free and embrace the woman she was meant to be. And Amelia knew, deep in her heart, that this was a battle she had to fight, a journey she had to take. The path ahead was uncertain, filled with fear and doubt, but it was also a path towards freedom, a journey of self-discovery that would lead her to a place she could only imagine.

A Call to Action

The familiar hum of the coffee shop was a soothing backdrop to Amelia's daily ritual. She sat in her usual corner booth, the worn leather cushioning her back, the scent of roasted beans mingling with the faint aroma of cinnamon from the bakery next door. It was a routine she'd cherished since moving to the city five years ago – a haven of normalcy amidst the whirlwind of her life.

Today, however, the routine felt suffocating, a stark contrast to the restlessness stirring deep within her. Her reflection in the polished surface of the coffee table seemed alien, the carefully crafted image of the 'good girl' she'd meticulously cultivated staring back at her. The 'good girl' who never raised her voice, who always smiled, who followed the rules, and who never, ever, strayed from the path laid out before her.

The city itself, once a vibrant tapestry of possibility, was now a canvas of sameness. The streets she'd once navigated with the thrill of exploration now felt like a familiar script, a repetitive loop playing out on an endless cycle. She was a character in a story that wasn't hers, a pawn in a game she'd never chosen to play.

The morning sun, filtering through the windowpanes, illuminated the crumpled newspaper on the table. A headline, "Women Still Struggle for Equality," caught her eye. The words triggered a wave of frustration, a simmering anger she'd kept bottled up for far too long.

"Equality? For who?" she whispered to herself, the question echoing in the quiet of the cafe. She wasn't just fighting for equality; she was fighting for the right to be herself, to break free from the chains of societal expectations and religious doctrines that had defined her existence for so long.

A wave of yearning washed over her, a longing for something more, something raw and untamed, and something that resonated with the rebellious spirit she'd buried deep within. She was tired of playing the role of the perfect daughter, the exemplary employee, the dutiful friend. She yearned to shed the mask and embrace the chaos that lurked beneath.

The cafe door opened, letting in a blast of cold air and a burst of energy that shattered the stillness of the morning. A woman with vibrant purple hair and a mischievous glint in her eye entered, her laughter ringing out like a siren song.

She was a kaleidoscope of color, her clothes a vibrant tapestry of patterns and textures, starkly contrasting Amelia's muted tones.

Amelia's gaze followed the woman as she made her way to the counter, her movements fluid and confident. The woman's presence was like a slap of reality, a reminder that life wasn't meant to be lived in shades of gray. It was meant to be a symphony of colors, a riot of experiences, and a journey of self-discovery.

As the woman ordered her coffee, her voice, a melody of confidence and whimsy, cut through the mundane conversation around her. Amelia watched, transfixed, a glimmer of hope flickering in her heart. This woman, this fearless individual, was a beacon in the darkness, a testament to the possibility of breaking free from the confines of expectations.

The woman's gaze met Amelia's, a knowing smile on her lips. "You look lost," she said, her voice a whisper in the bustling cafe. Amelia's heart skipped a beat, her cheeks flushed with embarrassment.

"I...I am," she stammered, unable to articulate the turmoil within.

The woman chuckled, her eyes sparkling with understanding. "We all are, at some point," she said, sitting across from Amelia. "But the magic is in the journey, the freedom to explore, to discover who we truly are. It's never too late to rewrite your story."

Amelia's mind raced, a torrent of questions and anxieties swirling. This woman, a stranger, had ignited a spark, a flicker of rebellion that had been dormant for far too long.

"How do you...how do you do it?" Amelia finally asked, her voice barely a whisper.

The woman took a sip of her coffee, her eyes twinkling with mischief. "You just have to dare to be yourself," she said, leaning forward, her voice dropping to a conspiratorial tone. "To embrace the chaos, to let go of the fear, and to dance with the wildness within. It's not always easy, but it's worth it. Trust me."

A wave of fear washed over Amelia, a familiar sensation of doubt and uncertainty. But beneath it, a spark of longing, a whisper of possibility, grew stronger. This woman, this stranger, had opened a door, offering a glimpse into a world beyond her comfort zone, a world where she could shed the mask and embrace the truth of who she was.

Amelia took a deep breath, a new determination settling in her chest. The city, once a symbol of confinement, now felt like a canvas of opportunity, a playground of possibilities waiting to be explored. The familiar routines, the comforting predictability, felt like a cage she was finally ready to escape.

She stood up, the chair scraping across the floor, a sound that seemed to echo her newfound resolve. "I'm going to do it," she said, her voice firm and resolute. "I'm going to find my way. I'm going to be free."

The woman smiled, a knowing glimmer in her eyes. "I knew you would," she said, her voice a whisper of encouragement.

As Amelia walked out of the cafe, the city lights blurring in her vision, she felt a weight lift from her shoulders, a sense of liberation that had been dormant for far too long. The path ahead was uncertain, filled with unknowns and challenges. But for the first time in her life, Amelia felt a sense of purpose, a sense of belonging, a sense of being finally, truly, free. The journey was just beginning, and she was ready to embrace it, all its wildness, all its beauty, all its terrifying, exhilarating truth.

Leaving the Familiar

The air in the quaint, suburban town where Amelia had always lived felt stifling. It wasn't just the humidity clinging to her skin, but the suffocating weight of expectations that had been pressed upon her since childhood. Her life, meticulously crafted according to the blueprints of her conservative upbringing and her family's unwavering religious beliefs, felt more like a gilded cage than a haven.

A yearning for something more, a primal urge to break free from the shackles of conformity, had been simmering within her for years. It began as a whisper, a faint echo of a different rhythm pulsing in the back of her mind. It was the feeling of being trapped in a costume, playing a role that felt increasingly foreign and uncomfortable. The "good girl" persona she had cultivated, the embodiment of all the virtues she'd been taught, was starting to feel like a mask, a carefully constructed facade hiding the complexities and contradictions simmering beneath the surface.

This desire for liberation manifested in subtle, almost imperceptible ways. A glance at a magazine with a daring fashion spread, a fleeting interest in a song with lyrics that hinted at forbidden desires, a stolen glance at a stranger who seemed to radiate a kind of unbridled freedom. These were the tiny cracks in the armor, the whispers that refused to be silenced, and the embers of rebellion that had been ignited in her heart.

One humid summer evening, as she sat on her porch swing, the scent of honeysuckle filling the air, she realized she couldn't ignore the whispers any longer. The feeling of being trapped, of living a life dictated by others, was unbearable. She longed for a life that felt true to herself, a life where she could explore the unexplored corners of her soul and embrace the parts of herself she had spent years suppressing.

The realization sparked a wildfire within her, a sudden burst of determination that fueled her with the courage to take a leap of faith. She had always dreamed of moving to a city, a place where anonymity would be a shield and where she could reinvent herself without the weight of judgment. The thought of leaving behind the familiar comforts of her life filled her with a mixture of exhilaration and terror, a sense of being teetering on the edge of a great abyss.

But the yearning for freedom was stronger than her fear. It was as if a dormant force had awakened within her, a force that demanded to be heard, and a force that whispered of endless possibilities waiting to be explored. In that moment, she made a decision, a decision that would alter the course of her life forever. She would leave the safety and security of her familiar world and venture into the unknown, embracing the uncertainty with open arms.

It was a radical choice, one that would inevitably shake the foundations of her life. She knew she was walking into the unknown, stepping onto a path that was paved with both opportunities and dangers. The "good girl" within her whispered warnings, cautioning her against the risks of straying from the familiar. But the voice of her true self, the one she had spent years ignoring, roared with excitement, urging her to embrace the adventure that lay ahead.

The decision to leave felt like a liberation, a shedding of a heavy burden she had carried for far too long. It was a declaration of independence, a refusal to be defined by the expectations of others. It was a moment of reckoning, a moment where she finally acknowledged the truth within her heart: she was not the "good girl" she had been taught to be, but a complex, multifaceted woman with a yearning for freedom, a desire for self-discovery, and a longing to explore the depths of her soul.

The city welcomed her with open arms, a vibrant tapestry of sights, sounds, and experiences unlike anything she had ever known. It was a place where she could shed the skin of her past and reinvent herself. With every step she took, with every new encounter, she felt the weight of expectations lifting, replaced by a sense of liberation she had never known before.

This was the beginning of her journey, a journey that would take her through unexpected twists and turns, leading her to confront her fears, embrace her desires, and discover the depths of her own power. It was a journey into the unknown, a journey that would ultimately lead her to find her true self, the one who had been hidden beneath the layers of societal expectations and internalized beliefs. It was a journey that would awaken the unbound soul within her.

Confronting Internal Conflict

The air in the quaint coffee shop was thick with the aroma of freshly brewed coffee and the murmur of hushed conversations. Amelia sat at a corner table, her latte growing cold as she stared out the window, a world of possibilities swirling in her head. The decision she had made, a decision that felt both exhilarating and terrifying, had finally taken root. Leaving behind the comfortable but stifling life she had meticulously crafted, she had embarked on a journey that was equal parts exhilarating and unsettling.

The journey had begun with a whisper, a growing dissatisfaction within her that she had initially tried to ignore. The life she had led, the "good girl" persona she had carefully cultivated, was starting to feel like a gilded cage. It was a life built on expectations, on fulfilling the roles that society had carved out for her. But deep inside, a yearning for something more, something truer, was slowly awakening.

The "good girl" Amelia had been taught to be – dutiful, obedient, and always striving to please – felt like a mask she was wearing, a persona that concealed the woman she truly was. This other woman, the one who yearned for liberation and self-expression, was now demanding to be seen, to be heard. She was the "bad girl," the rebellious spirit who whispered of forbidden desires and a life untamed.

The "good girl" clung to the familiar, to the safety of the life she knew. She warned Amelia of the dangers of venturing outside the lines, of the consequences of defying expectations. The "bad girl," however, was a siren, beckoning Amelia with promises of freedom, of a life lived on her own terms.

The clash between these two personas was an internal battleground, a constant tug-of-war that played out in her mind. It was a battle between comfort and courage, between conformity and authenticity. One voice urged her to stay within the boundaries, to maintain the facade, to continue playing the role that had been scripted for her. The other voice, the "bad girls" voice, urged her to break free, to shed the mask, to embrace the woman she was meant to be.

The conflict was not just within her; it was reflected in the world around her. The city she had left behind, with its rigid social structures and its unspoken rules, seemed to embody the "good girl" she had known. The new city she had arrived in, with its vibrant energy and its embrace of individuality, felt like a playground for the "bad girl" waiting to be unleashed.

In the city's bustling streets, she encountered individuals who mirrored her inner turmoil. Some were living embodiments of the "good girl" archetype – polished, successful, and seemingly content with their lives. Others were the living, breathing representations of the "bad girl" – unapologetically themselves, unafraid to embrace their desires and their flaws.

As Amelia navigated this new world, she found herself drawn to the "bad girls." Their free spirit, their defiance of expectations, their unwavering commitment to their truth, both intrigued and intimidated her. In their eyes, she saw a reflection of her yearning for liberation, a vision of the woman she could become.

Their presence stirred something within her, a sense of possibility, a glimmer of hope that maybe, just maybe, she could shed the "good girl" persona and embrace the woman she had always longed to be. But the fear lingered, a constant undercurrent of doubt that whispered in the back of her mind.

It was during one of these encounters, a chance meeting at a local art gallery, that she found herself drawn to a woman who radiated a confidence she had never experienced before. The woman, with her vibrant red hair, piercing blue eyes, and a rebellious spirit that exuded from every pore, was living proof that defying expectations was not only possible but empowering.

The woman, whose name was Luna, had a way of seeing through Amelia's facade, of recognizing the "bad girl" hidden beneath the surface. She encouraged Amelia to embrace her true self, let go of the fear, and explore the desires she had buried for so long. Luna's words were like a spark igniting a long- dormant flame, awakening within Amelia a sense of possibility she had thought was lost.

"Don't let them tell you who you are," Luna had said, her voice a blend of strength and compassion. "You have the power to define your own life, to create your own story. Don't be afraid to be bold, to be different, and to be truly you."

Amelia left the gallery that night with a newfound sense of determination. The journey ahead would be challenging, filled with uncertainties and internal conflicts. But she was no longer afraid. The "bad girl" within her was starting to awaken, and with each step forward, she felt a growing sense of liberation, a sense of freedom she had never known before.

The journey had just begun, and she was ready to face the unknown. The "good girl" persona, once so ingrained in her identity, was starting to fade. The "bad girl" was emerging, and with her came a sense of liberation and self- discovery that promised to change her life forever.

Early Encounters

The city thrummed with a vibrant energy that Amelia found both intoxicating and unsettling. Leaving her familiar, if stifling, life behind had been a leap of faith, a decision fueled by a potent mix of desperation and a burgeoning sense of self. As she navigated the bustling streets, a kaleidoscope of faces swirled around her, each one representing a potential path, a possible encounter that could shape her journey.

One afternoon, while browsing a vintage bookstore nestled in a quiet corner of the city, Amelia found herself drawn to a charismatic woman with a mischievous glint in her eye. The woman, named Luna, was a free spirit, her words flowing like a stream of consciousness, weaving tales of adventures and explorations of the human experience. Amelia, captivated by Luna's energy, found herself drawn into a conversation that stretched into the evening.

Luna, with her intoxicating blend of wisdom and wildness, became a guiding light for Amelia. She introduced her to a world where self-expression reigned supreme, where embracing the darker corners of one's psyche wasn't a sign of weakness but a source of power. Amelia learned about the importance of questioning societal norms, of challenging the expectations that had been imposed upon her since childhood. Luna, with her infectious laughter and unconventional wisdom, helped Amelia to see that her own desires, even the ones she had deemed unacceptable, held the key to true liberation.

Another encounter, far more jarring, took place at a local bar where Amelia stumbled upon a group of women who represented a different side of the coin. They were loud and defiant, their laughter tinged with an edge of cynicism. The conversation, fueled by cheap liquor and a potent cocktail of frustration and resentment, veered into territory Amelia found both unsettling and strangely alluring. They spoke openly about the injustices they had endured, the ways in which society had tried to silence and control them. Amelia, initially uncomfortable with their aggressive tone, found herself drawn to their raw honesty, their refusal to be silenced.

The leader of the group, a woman named Raven, was a force of nature. Her piercing gaze seemed to see through Amelia, exposing the inner turmoil she had been carrying for so long. Raven challenged Amelia's ingrained beliefs about "goodness" and "badness," suggesting that these labels were nothing more than constructs designed to control and manipulate women. She challenged Amelia to confront the fear that had kept her trapped, to embrace the shadows within and reclaim her power.

Amelia, caught between the warmth of Luna's wisdom and the raw intensity of Raven's rebellion, found herself at a crossroads. She was no longer the naive young woman who had accepted the "good girl" persona as her destiny. The encounters with these two women, so different yet both deeply compelling, had awakened a new hunger within her, a desire to break free from the chains of societal expectations and to explore the uncharted territories of her own soul.

One evening, while walking along the bustling streets of the city, Amelia noticed a small, unassuming bookstore tucked away in a dimly lit alleyway. Drawn by an inexplicable pull, she entered, the scent of old paper and ink filling her senses. As she browsed the shelves, she discovered a dusty, leather-bound volume titled "The Alchemist." The title intrigued her, and she couldn't resist picking it up. Flipping through the pages, she discovered a world filled with ancient wisdom, a journey of self-discovery that echoed the yearnings she had been carrying within her.

The book spoke of the importance of following one's dreams, of listening to the whispers of the soul and trusting in the universe's guiding hand. It spoke of the alchemist within each of us, the power we hold to transform our lives and our experiences. As Amelia absorbed the words on the page, she felt a shift within herself, a newfound sense of possibility, a belief that she could shape her own destiny, that she could, in fact, become the alchemist of her own life.

This encounter with "The Alchemist" became a pivotal moment in Amelia's journey. It fueled her desire for self-discovery, offering a map for the journey ahead. She began to see her own life as a tapestry woven with threads of both darkness and light, a story waiting to be written, a world waiting to be explored.

The encounters with Luna, Raven, and the enigmatic "The Alchemist" were just the beginning. Amelia's journey of self-discovery was just starting, and the city, with its endless possibilities, was the perfect setting for her transformation. She was ready to embrace the unknown, to explore the depths of her own desires, and to reclaim the power that had been hidden within her for so long.

The city was a canvas, a tapestry of experiences waiting to be woven into the story of her life. She was ready to start painting, to embrace the darkness and the light, to discover the woman she was truly meant to be.

The First Steps towards Embracing Her True Self

The scent of cinnamon and nutmeg filled the air as Amelia stood in her kitchen, the familiar aroma a grounding presence amidst the storm brewing within her. She had been making the same apple pie for years, the recipe handed down from her grandmother, a woman who believed in the power of tradition and the importance of a "good girl" life. But lately, the sweetness of the pie felt cloying, the cinnamon a bitter reminder of the expectations that had always felt like a tightrope walk.

The "good girl" life – it had been her blueprint, her compass, her shield. It meant following the rules, staying within the lines, keeping her desires neatly tucked away in a drawer labeled "Forbidden." It meant living a life that was predictable, safe, and acceptable. But something had shifted within her, an awakening that whispered of a different path, a path less traveled, a path that led to a woman she hadn't dared to imagine.

It started subtly, with a flicker of longing that she couldn't quite place. She caught herself staring at a woman in a coffee shop, captivated by the way she exuded confidence and joy, a stark contrast to the quiet reserved demeanor Amelia had cultivated. She found herself drawn to books about women who broke societal norms, women who defied expectations, women who embraced their sensuality and power.

The whispers of curiosity grew into a yearning, a desire to understand the woman she saw reflected in those stories, the woman she sensed simmering beneath the surface of her own life. It was a terrifying yet exhilarating feeling, like a moth drawn to a flickering flame, knowing it might be consumed yet unable to resist the pull.

One evening, Amelia found herself at a local art gallery, drawn by an exhibition featuring powerful female artists. The raw emotion and self-expression poured from the canvases, each brushstroke a rebellion against the constraints of traditional art. She stood before a painting of a woman with piercing blue eyes, her expression a mix of vulnerability and defiance, and a sudden wave of recognition washed over her.

This was the woman Amelia had been trying to ignore, the woman she had suppressed under the weight of expectations. This was the woman who yearned to break free from the cage she had built for herself, the woman who longed to explore the depths of her own desires.

Amelia started small. She enrolled in a pottery class, the feel of cool clay in her hands a calming presence. She discovered a passion for creating, each piece she molded a testament to her own unique expression. She joined a hiking club, pushing her boundaries, reveling in the feeling of freedom as she climbed mountain trails, the wind whipping through her hair, the world a canvas of vibrant color.

She began to experiment with her wardrobe, buying clothes that felt bold and daring, colors that screamed defiance against the muted tones she had always chosen. She found herself drawn to music that resonated with her newfound sense of liberation, lyrics that spoke of heartbreak and passion, of the raw power of vulnerability.

She even started to voice her opinions, even if it made her uncomfortable. She spoke up at work, challenging a sexist comment, the heat rising in her cheeks, but a newfound confidence fueling her words. She initiated conversations with friends, expressing her thoughts and feelings, her voice gaining strength with each sentence.

It was a journey of small but significant steps, each one pushing her closer to the woman she longed to be. It wasn't easy. The fear of judgment, the pull of familiar comfort, the whispers of guilt still lingered. But with each step, Amelia felt a sense of empowerment, a sense of liberation, a sense of reclaiming her own agency.

She was still a work in progress, a tapestry woven with threads of fear and doubt, but she was starting to see the beautiful, intricate pattern emerging. The "good girl" was still a part of her, but she was no longer defined by her. She was becoming a kaleidoscope of colors, a symphony of voices, a woman who was embracing the complexity and beauty of her own being.

Amelia looked at her reflection in the kitchen window, the light of the setting sun casting a golden glow on her face. She saw a glimmer of something new, something wild, something exhilarating. She knew she was only at the beginning of her journey, but for the first time in her life, she felt a sense of hope, a sense of possibility, a sense of liberation that filled her with an unknown but intoxicating joy. This was the beginning of her journey, the first steps towards embracing her true self, and the woman she had always been but had never allowed herself to be. And she was ready to embrace the journey, with all its complexities and contradictions, with a newfound sense of courage and a heart full of hope.

The Power of Choice

The wind whipped Amelia's hair around her face as she stood on the edge of the pier, staring out at the vast expanse of the ocean. The salty air stung her nostrils, a stark contrast to the sterile, predictable scent of her old life. She felt a deep, primal connection to the raw power of the sea, a feeling that mirrored the chaotic yet liberating storm raging within her. For months, she had been trapped in a gilded cage of her own making, a cage built from the expectations of her upbringing, the dictates of her religious community, and the societal norms that had shaped her identity.

But the cracks in the cage had begun to widen, revealing a yearning for something more, something beyond the confines of her carefully curated "good girl" persona. She had always played the role of the dutiful daughter, the exemplary student, the perfect wife. She had excelled at fulfilling the expectations placed upon her, but deep down, she knew this wasn't who she truly was. The life she lived was a carefully constructed facade, a mask she wore to appease her family, her community, and most importantly, herself.

She had been taught that her worth was measured by her obedience, her purity, her commitment to a life of conformity. Her desires, her passions, her yearning for something more were dismissed as frivolous, even dangerous. Yet, the seeds of rebellion had been planted, watered by a quiet longing that she could no longer ignore. The catalyst had been a chance encounter, a fleeting moment of connection with a woman who radiated a confidence and a freedom that Amelia had only ever dreamt of. This woman, with her vibrant energy and unfiltered honesty, had shown Amelia a glimpse of a life beyond the confines of her own self-imposed limitations.

It was a terrifying and exhilarating realization. Fear coiled around her heart, whispering of the consequences, the judgment, the potential for ruin. Yet, a newfound sense of urgency surged within her, a desperate need to break free from the chains that had bound her for so long. This wasn't just a desire for change, it was a fundamental shift in her understanding of herself. She realized that she wasn't simply trapped by external forces, but by her own internalized beliefs, the self-imposed limitations she had accepted as her truth.

Amelia began to question everything she had been taught, everything she had believed. The weight of expectations, the fear of judgment, the suffocating pressure to conform – these were the chains that held her captive, not the physical constraints of her environment. She started to see the world with fresh eyes, noticing the subtle ways societal expectations shaped her choices, her actions, her very sense of self. The "good girl" she had presented to the world was a carefully constructed facade, a mask designed to protect herself from the judgment of others, but in the process, it had also caged her own true self.

The realization hit her like a wave, crashing against the shore of her carefully constructed life. She could no longer ignore the yearning for liberation, the whispers of her own desires, the pull towards something more. A new purpose began to solidify within her, a burning desire to break free from the cage of expectations and embrace the woman she was truly meant to be. This journey, she knew, would be fraught with challenges, with internal conflicts and external resistance. But she was determined to confront her fears, to break through the walls she had built, and to step into the unknown.

This wasn't about abandoning her past, about rejecting the values that had shaped her. This was about reclaiming her power, about embracing her own truth, about finding her own path in a world that seemed to have already defined her destiny. She was no longer bound by the expectations of others, by the limitations of societal norms, by the fear of judgment. She had the power to choose her own path, to define her own life, to become the woman she was meant to be. This journey was about shedding the skin of the "good girl," embracing the "bad girl," and discovering the woman who resided in between, a woman who was both beautiful and fierce, vulnerable and strong, a woman who was truly, authentically herself.

The first step was a small one, a decision to take a leap of faith and step outside of her comfort zone. She booked a one-way ticket to a distant city, a place where she knew no one, a place where she could start anew, free from the whispers of her past, free from the judgment of her community. The fear was still there, a constant companion, but now it was eclipsed by a fierce determination, a burning desire to embrace the unknown and to finally become the woman she was meant to be.

The journey had just begun, and as Amelia boarded the plane, she felt a sense of both trepidation and exhilaration. The world was vast and full of possibilities, and she was ready to explore them all. The woman she was becoming was not defined by the "good girl" or the "bad girl," she was a mosaic of experiences, a tapestry of contradictions, a woman who was forever evolving, forever changing, forever becoming. And as she soared above the clouds, leaving the life she knew behind, Amelia knew that her journey to self-discovery had only just begun.

She arrived in the city with a suitcase full of clothes and a heart full of trepidation. The air buzzed with a frenetic energy, a chaotic symphony of honking horns, street vendors hawking their wares, and the incessant hum of city life. It was a far cry from the quiet, predictable life she had left behind, and it both terrified and invigorated her.

She had chosen to stay in a small, cozy guesthouse, a place that felt like a refuge amidst the chaos of the city. Her room was small, but it was her own, a sanctuary where she could finally breathe without the weight of expectations pressing down on her. The walls were adorned with vibrant paintings and framed photographs, each telling a story of the people who had passed through this place, leaving behind a whisper of their journeys.

Amelia spent the first few days simply exploring her new surroundings, allowing herself to be swept away by the energy of the city, to soak in the sights and sounds and smells that were so different from her old life. She wandered through bustling markets, marveling at the vibrant colors and exotic aromas, listened to street musicians playing their melodies, and watched children playing in the parks, their laughter echoing through the streets.

One afternoon, she found herself drawn to a small, independent bookstore nestled in a quiet corner of the city. The aroma of old books and the gentle hum of conversation filled the air as she stepped inside. The shelves were crammed with books of all genres, their spines whispering stories of adventure, love, and the complexities of the human experience. Amelia browsed the shelves, her fingers tracing the titles, her heart yearning for a connection, a story that would resonate with the journey she was on.

She stumbled upon a book titled "The Unbound Soul," a collection of essays by women who had defied expectations, embraced their own truth, and found their own path to liberation. The words leaped from the page, their stories resonating with the chaos and uncertainty that Amelia felt within herself. It was as if the author had tapped into her thoughts, her fears, her desires, and offered her a mirror to her own journey.

She bought the book, eager to dive into the words that offered her a sense of belonging, a reminder that she was not alone in her quest for self-discovery. As she settled into a comfy armchair in a corner of the bookstore, she began to read, each word a beacon of hope, a reminder that she had the power to choose her own destiny, to define her own life, to become the woman she was meant to be.

The essays spoke of the challenges of breaking free from societal expectations, of the internal conflicts that arose when one dared to step outside of the prescribed roles, of the fear of judgment and the courage it took to embrace one's own truth. They shared stories of love, loss, and the journey of self-discovery, of reclaiming their bodies, their voices, and their power. Their words resonated with Amelia, a chorus of voices echoing her own internal struggle, her own yearning for liberation.

As she read, Amelia began to see the world with fresh eyes, noticing the ways in which women were constantly being defined by others, their choices limited by societal expectations, their desires silenced by the weight of tradition and judgment. It was a world where the "good girl" was praised, while the "bad girl" was condemned, a world where women were expected to conform to pre- determined roles, to sacrifice their own desires for the sake of societal expectations. But these women, in their essays, defied those expectations, they embraced their own truth, they claimed their own power.

Amelia felt a sense of kinship with these women, a shared understanding of the struggles and triumphs of navigating a world that often felt hostile to their desires. Their stories offered her a sense of hope, a reminder that she was not alone in her quest for liberation, that it was possible to break free from the chains of societal expectations, to embrace her own truth, to become the woman she was meant to be.

As she read, Amelia's heart began to beat faster, her mind buzzing with new ideas, her spirit ignited by the possibilities that lay before her. She realized that her journey to self-discovery was not just about breaking free from the expectations of others, but about reclaiming her own agency, her own power, her own voice. She was not simply a daughter, a wife, a friend, she was a complex, multifaceted being with a story to tell, a life to live, a world to explore.

She closed the book, her mind racing, her heart overflowing with a newfound sense of purpose. This was not just a journey to self-discovery, it was a revolution, a rebellion against the limitations that had been imposed on her, a declaration of her own freedom. She had the power to choose her own path, to define her own life, to become the woman she was meant to be, and she was ready to embrace the journey, to face the challenges, to celebrate the triumphs, and to discover the woman who resided within, a woman who was both beautiful and fierce, vulnerable and strong, a woman who was truly, authentically herself.

As the sun dipped below the horizon, casting a warm glow over the city, Amelia walked back to her guesthouse, her heart overflowing with a newfound sense of hope. The journey was long and uncertain, but she was no longer afraid. She had found her voice, her power, her purpose. And as she stepped into the quiet sanctuary of her room, she knew that the woman she was becoming was a force to be reckoned with, a woman who was ready to claim her own liberation, to embrace her own truth, and to live a life that was truly her own.

Exploring the Forbidden

The air thrummed with a pulsating energy, a low vibration that resonated deep within Amelia's core. The city, once a canvas of sterile, predictable routines, now felt alive, throbbing with an unspoken rhythm that mirrored her own awakening desires. Stepping out of her comfort zone, she had embraced the unknown, venturing into uncharted territory where the boundaries of her carefully constructed world blurred and shifted.

A chance encounter with a woman named Anya, a whirlwind of vibrant energy and uninhibited spirit, had sparked a fire within her. Anya, a free spirit who reveled in the thrill of exploration, had introduced Amelia to a world where sexuality was not a shameful secret but a celebration of the body and its desires.

Amelia found herself drawn to Anya's effortless confidence, her uninhibited embrace of pleasure. She had never known a woman like Anya, someone who spoke openly about her desires, who didn't shy away from the raw, visceral power of her sensuality. It was both terrifying and exhilarating. Anya's unapologetic nature made Amelia question everything she thought she knew about herself and her place in the world.

Their first encounter, a night out at a dimly lit jazz club, had felt like a dream. As the music filled the room, weaving its magic through the air, Amelia found herself surrendering to a newfound sense of freedom. Anya's gaze, a mix of playful mischief and genuine warmth, had sent shivers down her spine. The way she moved, swaying with the rhythm, had awakened something primal within Amelia.

Anya's touch was electric, a gentle caress that sent a surge of heat through Amelia's veins. She had never felt so alive, so connected to her own body. The unspoken language of their shared gaze, a silent acknowledgment of their mutual attraction, had fueled a growing anticipation.

As the night progressed, they danced together, their bodies moving in sync with the music, a silent conversation unfolding between them. The world around them faded away, their focus narrowing to the intoxicating sensation of their intertwined bodies, the rhythmic pulse of their heartbeats echoing the pulsating bass.

In that moment, Amelia felt a liberation she had never known before. She was no longer the "good girl" she had always been, the one who followed the rules, who kept her desires safely locked away. She was a woman who was beginning to understand the power of her own sensuality, a woman who was willing to explore the forbidden realms of her desires.

Anya's presence was a catalyst, a spark that ignited a fire that had been simmering beneath the surface for years. She opened a door that Amelia had long kept closed, leading her to a world of sensuality she had only dared to imagine.

The journey was not without its challenges. As Amelia began to explore her sexuality, she faced a torrent of conflicting emotions. She grappled with the shame and guilt she had internalized for years, the societal messages that had painted sexuality as something to be feared and hidden.

The whispers of her upbringing, the strict religious teachings that had warned of the dangers of lust and sin, resonated in the back of her mind, creating a constant undercurrent of anxiety. She questioned everything she thought she knew about herself, her desires, and the very essence of her womanhood.

But amidst the internal conflict, a glimmer of liberation began to emerge. Anya's unwavering acceptance, her celebration of Amelia's awakening desires, offered a safe space for her to explore her sensuality without judgment. Anya's passion was contagious, her uninhibited joy a reminder that pleasure was not something to be feared but embraced.

Their relationship, a whirlwind of exhilarating encounters and raw emotions, became a crucible where Amelia forged a new understanding of herself. She began to understand that her sexuality was not something to be defined by societal norms or religious dictates. It was a part of her being, a source of power and pleasure that she could explore and claim as her own.

In the privacy of their shared moments, Amelia learned to connect with her own sensuality. She explored her body, discovering the subtle nuances of her desires, embracing the pleasure that unfolded within her. She learned to trust her own intuition, to listen to the whispers of her body, and to find delight in the sensations that arose within her.

The weight of societal expectations, the internalized messages of shame and guilt, started to loosen their grip. Anya's presence, a constant reminder of her own inherent worthiness, empowered Amelia to shed the layers of conditioning that had stifled her for so long.

As Amelia embraced her sensuality, she discovered a new sense of freedom and self-acceptance. She began to speak her truth, expressing her desires with a newfound confidence. She no longer felt the need to apologize for her wants or to hide her true self from the world.

The world felt different now, its colors more vibrant, and its sounds more alive. Every encounter, every interaction, was infused with a new layer of awareness. She was no longer the passive observer, the "good girl" who blended into the background. She was a woman who had claimed her power, a woman who was actively shaping her own destiny.

Amelia's journey was just beginning, but she knew that she was on the right path. The dance of desire, a journey of self-discovery and liberation, had only just begun. And with each step she took, she felt a growing sense of exhilaration, a sense of being fully alive, and a sense of finally coming home to herself.

The Shame and Guilt

The guilt was a heavy cloak, a suffocating weight that pressed down on Amelia's chest, constricting her breath. Every surge of desire, every flicker of pleasure, was met with a torrent of shame. The whispers of society, the pronouncements of her upbringing, echoed in her ears, a relentless chorus of condemnation. "Good girls don't do that," they chanted, their voices laced with judgment and disapproval. Amelia had always prided herself on being a good girl, the epitome of respectability, a daughter who never strayed from the path of righteousness. Now, she found herself drowning in a sea of contradictions, her carefully constructed persona crumbling under the weight of newfound desires.

How could she, a woman who had always embodied virtue, find herself consumed by thoughts that felt so...wrong? She was no longer a girl, but she was still grappling with the societal messages she had internalized since childhood. Her body, once a vessel of purity and innocence, was now a source of both pleasure and torment. The sensations she had learned to suppress, the desires she had buried deep within, were now bubbling to the surface, demanding recognition. But how could she reconcile these feelings with the "good girl" she had always believed herself to be?

Amelia found herself caught in a vicious cycle. She would crave intimacy, the raw and unbridled connection that whispered promises of ecstasy. But as soon as she felt the heat of desire rising within her, a wave of guilt would wash over her, dragging her back to the safety of her carefully constructed cage. The voice of her past, the echoes of societal expectations, would drown out the whispers of her true self.

She would dismiss her desires as fleeting urges, mere aberrations that were not truly a part of who she was.

The shame, like a relentless shadow, followed her everywhere. It clung to her like a second skin, reminding her of her supposed transgressions, of the ways in which she had fallen short of the "good girl" ideal. It was a silent tormentor, whispering doubts and insecurities into her ear, fueling her self-recrimination. Every encounter, every touch, every fleeting glance, was tinged with a sense of wrongness. She couldn't escape the feeling that she was betraying something, someone, even though she wasn't quite sure what or who.

Amelia sought solace in isolation, attempting to bury her desires under a mountain of self-denial. She would spend hours poring over religious texts, seeking answers to her internal conflict. But the words on the page seemed to mock her, offering no comfort, no release. The scriptures that had once offered a sense of purpose and guidance now seemed empty, their pronouncements failing to resonate with her experience. She found herself questioning the very foundation of her beliefs, wondering if she had been living a lie.

Her internal conflict manifested in physical ways as well. She felt a constant tension in her body, a tightness in her chest that made it difficult to breathe. Her sleep was troubled, filled with disturbing dreams that mirrored the turmoil raging within her. Even the simple act of eating became a challenge, the food losing its appeal as her mind raced with self-doubt and self-recrimination.

Amelia was trapped in a prison of her own making, her mind a battleground where conflicting ideologies waged war. The "good girl" she had so meticulously crafted, the persona she had presented to the world, was now crumbling before her eyes. The "bad girl," the woman she had suppressed for so long, was demanding her freedom, her voice growing louder with every passing day. But how could Amelia reconcile these conflicting sides of herself? How could she embrace the desires that made her feel so conflicted and ashamed?

The weight of the world, of societal expectations and internalized beliefs, pressed down on her. Amelia longed to break free from the shackles of shame, to dance with her desires without fear of judgment. But the journey ahead seemed daunting, fraught with uncertainty and the lingering threat of guilt.

She began to question everything she thought she knew about herself, about her sexuality, about the world around her. She started to understand that the shame she felt was not her own, but a reflection of a society that was still struggling to reconcile its own internal conflict about female sexuality.

The guilt, the shame, the fear, they were all intertwined, a tangled web that she desperately wanted to unravel. But the truth was, she didn't know where to start. The journey to self-acceptance seemed insurmountable, the path ahead obscured by the fog of her own doubt.

As Amelia stared at her reflection, she saw a woman who was both familiar and alien. The "good girl" she had always known was fading, revealing a stranger beneath. A woman who craved freedom, who longed to express her desires without fear or shame. But could she truly embrace this unknown woman, this "bad girl" who was slowly coming to light? Or would the weight of societal expectations and internalized beliefs continue to hold her captive, leaving her forever caught in the dance of desire?

Finding Pleasure and Empowerment

The air in the room was thick with the scent of jasmine and the soft, sultry melody of a jazz record playing on Amelia's vintage record player. She had always loved jazz, the way it swayed and flowed, echoing the rhythm of her own heartbeat. Tonight, though, the music felt different, more intimate, and more personal. It was as though the notes were whispering secrets, urging her to let go, to explore, to discover.

Amelia lay on the plush velvet rug, her bare body curled against the cool, smooth wood of her antique dresser. She had been reading a book about female pleasure, something she had always shied away from, afraid of the shame and judgment that seemed to cling to the topic like a shroud. But tonight, something had shifted within her. The whispers of the music, the soft glow of candlelight, the weight of her own desire – it was all coming together, creating a symphony of longing and awakening.

For years, Amelia had been conditioned to believe that pleasure was something to be reserved for a partner, something to be earned, something to be ashamed of. She had lived her life as a "good girl," carefully curating her image, her actions, and her thoughts, to fit within the confines of societal expectations. But tonight, a new wave of understanding washed over her.

Pleasure wasn't a reward or a concession. It wasn't something to be hidden or feared. It was a fundamental part of her being, an intrinsic right, a source of empowerment. As the music swelled around her,

Amelia closed her eyes and began to explore her own body, her fingers tracing the curves of her hips, the softness of her breasts, and the delicate pulse of her neck.

With each touch, a tremor of sensation ran through her, sending shivers down her spine. She felt a sense of wonder and curiosity, a newfound appreciation for the beauty and complexity of her own form. For the first time, she was experiencing pleasure not as a fleeting indulgence, but as a deep, abiding connection to her own sensuality.

The shame she had carried for so long began to recede, replaced by a sense of confidence and liberation. Amelia realized that her sexuality was not a sin or a weakness. It was a powerful force, a source of creation, a conduit for connection. She began to see her body not as an object to be judged or controlled, but as a sacred temple, a vessel for her own desires, and a conduit for her own pleasure.

Amelia's exploration took her beyond the physical. She started to delve into the realm of fantasy and imagination, letting her mind wander to places she had never dared to venture before. She imagined herself as a powerful goddess, embracing her strength and sensuality, claiming her desires with unwavering confidence. She imagined herself as a free spirit, dancing under a moonlit sky, feeling the wind through her hair, the earth beneath her feet.

The journey was not without its bumps. There were moments of doubt, whispers of fear, and the persistent echo of societal conditioning. But Amelia persevered, fueled by the newfound awareness of her own power and the unwavering desire to reclaim her pleasure. She sought out resources, conversations, and experiences that empowered her to understand and embrace her sexuality on her own terms.

She discovered a community of women who were also challenging the status quo, women who were reclaiming their voices, their bodies, and their desires. These women became her mentors, guides, and sisters in arms, sharing their stories, wisdom, struggles, and triumphs.

Amelia began to understand that pleasure wasn't just a physical sensation, but a state of being, a way of living, a way of claiming her power in the world. It was about understanding her own desires, honoring her own boundaries, and speaking her truth with unwavering confidence.

The jazz music continued to play, its melody weaving a tapestry of liberation and self-discovery. Amelia, no longer bound by the chains of societal expectations or the shackles of self-doubt, felt a surge of pure, unadulterated joy. She had begun to dance with her desire, embracing her sensuality, her power, her true self. And in the depths of that dance, she found a sense of peace, of freedom, of belonging. It was a journey that had just begun, but one that promised to lead her to a life that was authentic, fulfilling, and deeply pleasurable.

Reclaiming Her Voice

The bar, with its dim lighting and the rhythmic pulse of the bass, felt like a different world. It was a world Amelia had only glimpsed from afar, a world of whispered conversations and lingering glances, a world where desire was a palpable force. Tonight, she was stepping into that world, her heart pounding a frantic rhythm against her ribs.

The night was a symphony of senses. The scent of amber and sandalwood mixed with the faint sweetness of her cocktail. The warmth of the music vibrated through the floorboards, a steady rhythm that urged her to move, to lose herself in the beat. And then there was the touch, the accidental brush of a hand, the fleeting glance that sent a jolt of electricity through her veins.

It was exhilarating and terrifying all at once. The "good girl" in her, the one raised on the strict doctrines of faith and societal expectations, whispered warnings. But the "bad girl," the one who had been simmering beneath the surface, was finally ready to break free.

She found herself drawn to a man, a stranger with piercing blue eyes and a smile that promised both mischief and understanding. He seemed to sense her hesitation, her internal battle between the two sides of her being. His eyes, warm and inviting, held a knowing look that sent shivers down her spine. He spoke to her, his voice smooth and confident, and something within her loosened. The tension, the fear, began to dissipate.

As they talked, the words flowed freely, unfiltered by the self-censorship she had practiced for years. She found herself speaking of her desires, the things she had kept hidden even from herself. She spoke of the longing for connection, the yearning for something more than the safe, predictable life she had built.

He listened intently, his eyes reflecting a deep empathy that made her feel seen and understood. For the first time, she felt a sense of freedom, a liberation from the shackles of her self- imposed limitations. There was an unspoken understanding between them, a recognition of the shared human experience of desire and longing.

The night unfolded like a dream. The boundaries, the lines she had drawn around herself, dissolved in the heat of the moment. She allowed herself to be swept away by the rhythm of the music, by the intoxicating scent of his cologne, by the electric energy that flowed between them. The touch, initially tentative, became bolder, more intimate.

He kissed her, a slow, deliberate kiss that awakened something primal within her. For a moment, all the anxieties, the doubts, the whispers of judgment, faded into the background. It was only the two of them, lost in the dance of desire, two souls seeking connection, two hearts beating in unison.

But then, the reality of her world crashed back in. The whispers of the "good girl" returned, louder now, tinged with fear and self-recrimination. The words of her upbringing, the societal messages about morality and propriety, echoed in

Her head.

She pulled away, the kiss breaking like a fragile bubble. The warmth of the moment quickly dissipated, replaced by a chill of self-doubt and fear. She looked at him, a mixture of confusion and regret in her eyes. He saw the conflict reflected in her face, the flicker of fear that threatened to extinguish the spark between them.

"I'm sorry," she whispered, her voice shaky. "I can't."

He reached for her hand, his touch warm and comforting. "It's okay," he said softly. "There's no need to apologize."

She knew he was right. There was no need to apologize for her desires, for the exploration of her own sensuality. But the "good girl" still held her captive, whispering her own brand of truth. She needed time, she realized, to reconcile the conflicting sides of herself.

As she walked away, the music fading behind her, she felt a mixture of sadness and liberation. She had tasted freedom, a glimpse of a world where she could be her true self, without judgment or fear. And even though she had pulled back, she knew this was only the beginning.

The journey of self-discovery was messy, complicated, and often uncomfortable. But Amelia had taken the first step. She had tasted the forbidden fruit, and the knowledge it offered, though terrifying, was ultimately empowering. She knew, with a deep certainty, that her journey was just beginning. She would face the challenges, the internal conflicts, the whispers of shame and guilt. But she would do it with a newfound strength, a newfound understanding of her own desires, and a growing belief in her right to explore them.

The dance of desire had only just begun. And Amelia, with a heart full of both fear and excitement, was ready to dance.

Learning to Trust Herself

The air in the room was thick with the scent of jasmine and vanilla, a heady mix that seemed to amplify the emotions swirling within Amelia. She lay on the soft, silk sheets, her body languid and relaxed, yet a sense of unease lingered in her mind. It had been weeks since she had first ventured into the world of her desires, and the experience had been both exhilarating and terrifying. She had explored the depths of her sensuality, reveling in the pleasure and the power of her own body. Yet, amidst the intoxicating freedom, a nagging voice whispered doubts in her ear.

The voice, familiar from a lifetime of conditioning, questioned her choices, reminding her of the societal expectations she had always strived to meet. It accused her of betraying the "good girl" she had presented to the world, the image she had meticulously cultivated. The guilt it invoked was a heavy cloak, threatening to suffocate the newly awakened sense of self-expression.

Amelia found herself grappling with a conflict she had never anticipated. How could she reconcile the "good girl" with the "bad girl" she had discovered within? How could she embrace the pleasure and power of her own body without sacrificing the moral code she had always held dear? The questions gnawed at her, leaving her feeling vulnerable and exposed.

One afternoon, as she sat in a cafe, sipping a cup of coffee, she noticed a woman reading a book. The woman had a wild, untamed energy that radiated from her, a confidence that Amelia found both alluring and intimidating. Amelia, driven by a curiosity she couldn't quite ignore, approached her.

"Excuse me," Amelia began, her voice hesitant, "That book looks interesting. What is it about?"

The woman looked up, her eyes sparkling with a mischievous glint. "It's a story about a woman who discovers her power," she replied, her voice warm and inviting. "It's about reclaiming your voice, your body, your soul."

Amelia felt a jolt of recognition. It was as if the woman had seen into her soul, recognizing the internal struggle she had been battling. She found herself drawn to the woman's energy, the way she radiated a sense of freedom and self- acceptance.

"I'm Amelia," she introduced herself, feeling a surge of courage. "And I think I need to hear that story."

The woman smiled, "I'm Maya. Let's talk."

And so, Amelia began to pour out her heart, sharing her fears, her doubts, and the overwhelming sense of confusion she was experiencing. Maya listened patiently, offering words of encouragement and wisdom.

She reminded Amelia that her body and her sexuality were her own, and that she had the right to explore and express them freely.

"Your body is a temple," Maya said, her voice soft yet firm. "It's a source of power, pleasure, and creativity. It's not something to be ashamed of, but something to be cherished and celebrated."

Amelia had never heard anyone speak about her body in such a way. The words resonated deep within her, dispelling the layers of shame and guilt she had carried for so long. As Maya continued to share her story, Amelia felt a shift within her. The fear and doubt began to recede, replaced by a growing sense of empowerment.

"You are not defined by the 'good girl' persona you have created," Maya insisted, her eyes meeting Amelia's with unwavering conviction. "You are not defined by societal expectations or by the judgments of others. You are a complex, multifaceted being with a right to explore your own desires, to find your own path."

Amelia realized that Maya's words were not just words of encouragement, but a call to action. It was a call to trust herself, to listen to her own inner voice, and to reject the limiting beliefs that had held her captive for so long. She understood that the journey she had embarked upon was not about becoming a "bad girl" but about becoming her true self, embracing all the complexities and contradictions that made her uniquely her.

The fear was still there, but it no longer held the same power over her. It was replaced by a growing sense of curiosity, a desire to explore the depths of her own being without the shackles of guilt or shame. She began to listen more closely to her body, to her desires, and to trust the wisdom that resided within.

Amelia started to understand that the "good girl" and the "bad girl" were not separate entities but different facets of her own identity. She realized that the "good girl" persona she had cultivated was not inherently bad, but simply a reflection of the societal expectations she had internalized. She could embrace both her good and her bad, her light and her shadow, without feeling the need to choose one over the other.

The journey was far from over, but Amelia felt a growing sense of hope and liberation. She knew that she still had much to learn, much to unlearn, and much to explore. But she also knew that she had taken the first steps towards reclaiming her power, her sexuality, and her soul. And that was a truth worth embracing, a truth that promised a life of freedom, authenticity, and joy.

Confronting Past Trauma

The familiar scent of cinnamon and nutmeg, the aroma of my grandmother's baking, always transported me back to a time when life felt simple, innocent. But that innocence, that comforting sense of security, was shattered years ago, a shattered mirror that continued to reflect distorted fragments of my past. The image that lingered, a haunting specter in

My subconscious, was the night of the dance.

It wasn't the dance itself that had left a mark, but the aftermath. The whispers, the stares, the judgment etched in the eyes of my classmates. It had all started with a simple misunderstanding, a playful touch, a misplaced hand on my waist that was misinterpreted. I was a good girl, I always had been, and that single incident, that brief moment of physical intimacy, had irrevocably stained my reputation.

The whispers followed me everywhere, from the hushed corners of the school hallways to the Sunday service pews. I was the girl who had crossed the line, the girl who had dared to step outside the confines of the "good girl" box. The guilt, the shame, the fear of judgment, it consumed me.

In the aftermath of that night, a wall grew within me, an impenetrable barrier that guarded my vulnerabilities, my desires. It was as if I had been branded, marked with the scarlet letter of a transgression I didn't fully understand.

I had never been the "bad girl," not the rebellious type who dared to defy expectations. I had always strived for perfection, for the approval of my parents, my church, my community. But that night, the whispers had eroded my carefully constructed facade, leaving behind a fragile sense of self-worth.

I buried myself deeper into the "good girl" persona, clinging to it as a shield against the world's judgment. I suppressed my desires, my curiosity, my longing for something more. My sexuality, a hidden treasure buried beneath layers of shame and guilt, became a source of anxiety, a taboo topic that I dare not explore.

The memory of that night, of the whispers, the stares, the judgment, it continued to haunt me, whispering in my ear, reminding me of my supposed transgression. It became a narrative that shaped my beliefs about myself, about my sexuality, about my place in the world.

The "good girl" persona, once a source of comfort, had become a prison. It confined me, restricting my freedom to explore my true self, to embrace my desires, to live authentically.

I had spent years living in the shadow of that past, fearing the whispers, the judgments. But as I stood at the precipice of this new chapter in my life, I realized that it was time to confront the past, to break free from the prison of my own making.

I had a choice: I could continue to be haunted by the past, trapped in a self-imposed cage of shame and guilt. Or I could choose to heal, to reclaim my power, to liberate myself from the whispers.

The path ahead was uncertain, the journey fraught with challenges, but I was determined to face my demons head- on. I was determined to confront the uncomfortable truth, the truth of my past, the truth of my desires, the truth of who I truly was.

As I delved deeper into my past, I realized that the whispers, the judgment, they weren't about me. They were about the societal expectations that dictated how women should behave, how they should present themselves, how they should express their sexuality.

It was time to reclaim my narrative, to rewrite the story of my life. It was time to break free from the shackles of societal expectations and embrace the freedom to be my true self.

The path ahead was not easy, but I was determined to walk

It. I was determined to find my voice, to embrace my desires, to reclaim my power. I was determined to live a life that was authentic to me, a life that was free from the whispers, free from the judgment, free from the fear.

The journey began with a simple act of self-compassion, of recognizing the pain I had carried for so long. I started by understanding that the whispers, the judgment, they didn't define me. I was not the sum of my past mistakes. I was a woman with a story to tell, a woman who was worthy of love, acceptance, and freedom.

I sought solace in the writings of feminist authors, their words resonating with my own struggles. I found strength in the stories of other women who had broken free from the confines of societal expectations, who had dared to embrace their individuality and their desires.

Their voices echoed in my heart, reminding me that I was not alone, that there was a sisterhood of women who understood, who supported, and who celebrated the journey of self-discovery.

I began to explore my own sexuality with curiosity, with a sense of liberation. I was no longer afraid of the whispers, no longer afraid of the judgment. I was determined to explore my desires, to embrace my sensuality, to reclaim my power over my own body.

My journey was far from over, but each step forward, each act of self-acceptance, each moment of freedom, filled me with a sense of hope, a sense of liberation.

I was no longer the girl who had been branded by the whispers, the girl who had been defined by a single night. I was a woman who was finally embracing her truth, a woman who was finally finding her voice, a woman who was finally reclaiming her power.

The journey was ongoing, the path winding and unpredictable, but I had finally found the courage to step onto it, to walk towards the light, to break free from the shadows of the past.

The future held endless possibilities, and I was ready to embrace them all. I was ready to be unbound.

Healing and Acceptance

The weight of the past slammed onto Amelia's shoulders, a crushing reminder of the life she had so meticulously tried to bury. The trauma, shrouded in whispers and shame, rose like a specter from the depths of her memory. The whispers morphed into guttural screams, echoing the years of self- doubt and suppressed desires. The truth, as it always does, was uncomfortable, a jagged shard of reality piercing the carefully constructed facade of her life.

The "good girl" persona, the one she had so diligently cultivated, crumbled under the weight of this truth. It was a persona crafted from societal expectations, religious dogma, and the fear of stepping out of line. It was a cage she had built, brick by brick, to protect herself from the world, but also to stifle her own voice. The truth forced her to confront the pain she had been carrying, the pain that had shaped her beliefs about herself, about her sexuality, about her worth. It was a pain that had seeped into every facet of her being, a dark undercurrent that had dictated her choices, her relationships, and her very sense of self.

The realization was both terrifying and liberating. It was terrifying because it meant acknowledging the wounds that ran deep, the scars that had become a part of her. It was liberating because it meant she could finally begin to heal. The path ahead was fraught with challenges, but Amelia felt a surge of resolve. She would not let the past define her. She would not let the pain cripple her.

The first step was acknowledging the trauma. It was a painful process, a journey back into the darkest corners of her memory. The memories, once buried deep beneath layers

Of denial and self-blame, surfaced with a force that threatened to overwhelm her. She saw the faces of those who had hurt her, heard the words that had cut her deeply, felt the sting of betrayal and the weight of shame. She understood that she was not responsible for the actions of others, that

She had not deserved the pain she had endured.

The next step was seeking support. She reached out to a therapist, a safe space where she could finally unpack the years of baggage she had been carrying. The therapist listened without judgment, a beacon of compassion in the darkness. She helped Amelia understand the impact of trauma on her psyche, her relationships, and her sense of self. The therapist provided tools for healing, teaching Amelia how to navigate the emotional landscape, how to reclaim her power, and how to move forward with grace and resilience.

In addition to therapy, Amelia sought out healing practices that resonated with her. She found solace in nature, its beauty and peace a balm for her troubled mind. She started journaling, pouring her thoughts and feelings onto paper, allowing the words to release the tension held within her. She embraced the practice of mindfulness, learning to be present in the moment, to observe her thoughts and emotions without judgment, and to cultivate a sense of inner calm.

The healing process was not linear. There were days when the pain felt overwhelming, when the memories threatened to consume her. There

were moments of doubt and despair, when she questioned her ability to heal, to move beyond the pain. But she clung to the support she had found, to the tools she had learned, to the hope that she could reclaim her power and create a life that was free from the shackles of the past.

Slowly but surely, the healing began. The pain did not disappear overnight, but it became less intense, less consuming. She started to see glimpses of the woman she had been meant to be, a woman who was strong, resilient, and full of life. She started to feel a sense of agency, a sense of control over her own life, a sense of hope for the future.

The journey was long and winding, but with each step, Amelia felt a shift within her. She began to understand that healing was not about erasing the past, but about integrating it into her story, about learning from it, and about using it to fuel her growth. It was about reclaiming her power and finding her voice, about embracing her imperfections and celebrating her strengths, about creating a life that was true to her authentic self.

The uncomfortable truth had brought her to her knees, but it had also given her the strength to rise again, to stand tall, to finally step into her power.

Redefining Her Boundaries

The air hung heavy with unspoken words. Amelia sat across from her therapist, her gaze fixed on the intricate patterns of the rug beneath her feet. The therapist, a kind woman with eyes that seemed to hold a lifetime of wisdom, gently prodded Amelia to delve deeper into the recent breakdown of her relationship with Tom. Amelia had been dating Tom for almost two years, a seemingly perfect match on paper.

He was charming, successful, and everything her parents had always wanted for her. But the reality was far from idyllic. Tom, despite his outward charm, had a way of subtly controlling Amelia's life, chipping away at her sense of self- worth with passive-aggressive remarks and veiled criticisms. It was as if he possessed an invisible leash, tugging her back into his world whenever she dared to stray.

Amelia had always been the "good girl," the one who followed the rules and avoided confrontation. But as her relationship with Tom unraveled, she found herself questioning her lifelong commitment to pleasing others. The more she fought for her independence, the more Tom pushed back, making her feel guilty for wanting to explore her own desires. The realization that she had been allowing someone to diminish her sense of self was a painful pill to swallow.

"You're strong, Amelia," the therapist said softly, breaking through the wall of silence that had settled between them. "You're capable of setting healthy boundaries and protecting your own well-being. You just need to believe in yourself."

Amelia's eyes welled up. The therapist's words were a gentle echo of the whispers of rebellion that had been growing within her for months. She had always felt a deep-seated fear of disappointing the people around her, particularly her parents, who had instilled in her a strong sense of duty and obligation. But Tom's constant demands and subtle manipulations had forced her to confront the reality of her situation: she was allowing him to control her life because she was afraid of his disapproval.

The therapist continued, "Boundaries are not about being selfish; they are about respecting yourself and your needs. They are about creating a safe space for you to grow and flourish."

Those words resonated deep within Amelia. For the first time, she began to understand that setting boundaries wasn't about shutting people out but about creating a clear framework for healthy and respectful relationships. It was about asserting her own voice and claiming her right to prioritize her own well-being.

Amelia's journey towards self-discovery had begun with a slow, almost imperceptible shift in her perspective. The "good girl" persona she had cultivated for so long was slowly fading, revealing a woman who was both empowered and vulnerable.

It was a process that involved confronting the fears that had held her captive for years: the fear of disappointing her parents, the fear of rejection, and the fear of being perceived as selfish or demanding. But with each step, Amelia's confidence grew. She started to assert herself in small ways, speaking her truth, setting clear expectations, and saying "no" to requests that felt draining or disrespectful. The initial resistance, the internal guilt and fear, gradually subsided as she witnessed the positive impact of her actions. She began to recognize that her voice was not only valid but also powerful.

The process wasn't easy. There were moments of doubt, moments of fear, and moments when she wanted to retreat back to the comfort zone of compliance. But Amelia's resolve grew stronger with each challenge she faced. She realized that the true strength lay in her vulnerability, in her willingness to express her needs and desires, and in her commitment to protecting her own well-being.

The journey toward setting boundaries was a gradual one, a process of continuous learning and self-discovery. Amelia learned that boundaries weren't static but fluid, evolving alongside her own growth and understanding. She discovered that boundaries were not a means of isolating herself from others but rather a way of fostering deeper and more meaningful connections.

As Amelia continued to redefine her boundaries, she realized that it wasn't just about her relationships with others; it was also about her relationship with herself. She began to understand the importance of listening to her own intuition, respecting her own needs, and prioritizing her own happiness.

She discovered that true freedom wasn't about conforming to societal expectations but about embracing her own unique path, a path that might not always be easy but was ultimately her own. It was a path that led her to a deeper understanding of her own worth and a more authentic expression of her true self.

Amelia's journey towards redefining her boundaries was a testament to the power of self-discovery and the transformative nature of vulnerability. It was a journey that challenged her beliefs, pushed her beyond her comfort zone, and ultimately led her to a place of greater self-love and self- acceptance. It was a journey that reminded her that she was not defined by the expectations of others but by her own unique spirit, a spirit that was now free to soar.

The Strength in Vulnerability

Amelia's journey to self-discovery had been a relentless exploration of her deepest desires, a fearless plunge into the unknown. She'd traversed the terrain of her own suppressed desires, confronted the shame and guilt she'd carried for so long, and begun to claim her power. But there was still a layer, a deeply buried truth she'd yet to unearth. It lay dormant within her, a painful memory she'd locked away, fearing the emotional upheaval it would bring.

One day, as Amelia was walking through the park, the familiar scent of freshly cut grass and blooming lilacs triggered a wave of memories. It was the smell of her childhood home, the smell of innocence, but also the smell of something else, something darker. A sudden tightness constricted her chest, a feeling she hadn't experienced in years. She stopped, her breath catching in her throat, as a long-suppressed image surfaced in her mind.

It was a memory of a summer evening, a time when she was young and impressionable. A memory of an incident with a family friend, a man who had taken advantage of her vulnerability. It was a memory she had desperately tried to bury, a secret she had kept locked away for years, fearing judgment and shame.

But now, standing in the park, amidst the intoxicating scents of spring, the memory broke through the walls she had erected around it. It was like a dam bursting, releasing a torrent of emotions she'd been holding back for so long. She felt a surge of anger, a wave of sadness, and a profound sense of violation. It was a painful awakening, a confrontation with a truth she had been trying to outrun.

Tears streamed down Amelia's face as the memory replayed in her mind. She felt a deep sense of shame and guilt, a sense of being broken. She hadn't been strong enough to fight back, not at that age. She had allowed herself to be violated, and the shame of that experience had haunted her for years. It was a part of her story she'd tried to erase, a truth she'd hidden from herself.

But in that moment, amidst the lush greenery of the park, something shifted within her. She realized that she was not to blame. The incident had been a violation, an act of power exerted over a young and vulnerable girl. It was not her fault, and she did not have to carry the burden of shame any longer.

The weight of the memory, once suffocating, started to lift. It was like the sun breaking through dark clouds, casting a warm light on the world around her. She felt a surge of strength, a sense of determination to face the truth, to heal, and to move forward.

For the first time, Amelia understood the power of vulnerability. It wasn't weakness, it wasn't a sign of fragility. It was a testament to her courage, a testament to her ability

To face her deepest fears and to embrace the truth, even when it was painful. It was in her vulnerability that she found the strength to move forward.

Amelia realized that her journey had been leading her to this moment. The exploration of her sexuality, the reclaiming of her body, the shedding of societal expectations – all of it had been preparing her for this reckoning with her past. It had been a journey of self-discovery, but it was also a journey of healing.

She knew that the path ahead wouldn't be easy. She had to process the trauma, to forgive herself, and to find a way to integrate this painful memory into her life without letting it define her. It was a challenge, but one she was determined to face.

Amelia's journey was far from over, but in that moment, standing amidst the beauty of the park, she felt a new sense of hope. She had unearthed a painful truth, but in doing so, she had found a new level of strength and resilience. She had faced her vulnerability, and in doing so, she had discovered an extraordinary power within herself.

From that moment on, Amelia's journey took on a new dimension. She realized that healing was not about erasing the past, but about integrating it into the narrative of her life. She had to find a way to carry this burden, not with shame and guilt, but with strength and compassion.

She sought therapy, a safe space to talk about her experience without fear of judgment. She found a group of women who had also experienced trauma, sharing their stories and offering support and understanding. She learned that she was not alone in her pain, and that healing was possible, even from the deepest wounds.

Amelia also began to focus on self-care, nurturing her body and mind with healthy practices. She engaged in yoga, meditation, and journaling, all of which helped her to connect with her inner strength and to release the emotional tension she had been carrying for years.

The process of healing wasn't always easy, but Amelia was committed to the journey. She knew that the pain she had buried for so long would not disappear overnight, but she was determined to face it, to heal, and to emerge stronger on the other side.

One day, as Amelia was talking to her therapist about the progress she was making, she realized that the journey of healing wasn't just about confronting the past, but also about embracing the future. She was no longer the same girl who had been violated. She had grown, she had become stronger, and she had found her voice.

Amelia understood that her past experiences had shaped her, but they did not define her. She was a survivor, she was resilient, and she was ready to embrace the future with a newfound sense of freedom and self-love. She had found the strength in her vulnerability, and in doing so, she had unlocked a power within herself she had never known existed.

Her journey was far from over, but she was ready to continue on, carrying the weight of her past with courage and compassion, always striving to be her most authentic self.

Embracing Her Imperfections

The mirror reflected a woman she barely recognized. The smooth surface held a stranger, a woman whose eyes held a quiet intensity that had been absent before. Amelia, with her carefully constructed facade of "good girl," had always been a master of hiding her true self. But somewhere along the way, the cracks in the mask had grown too wide to ignore. The self she had so meticulously crafted for the world began to crumble, revealing the raw, unfiltered truth beneath.

The uncomfortable truth, however, was not a monster to be feared. Instead, it was a liberating revelation, a whispered promise of a life that resonated with authenticity. The imperfections she had so desperately tried to hide were the very elements that made her unique, the threads woven into the tapestry of her being. She had spent years striving for an unattainable standard of perfection, believing that her worth was contingent upon her ability to fit into a mold designed by society. But as the pieces of her carefully curated persona fell away, she began to see her imperfections as a badge of honor, a testament to her own unique journey.

The realization dawned on her in a wave of unexpected clarity. She was not defined by her flaws; she was defined by the way she embraced them. The anxieties, the insecurities, the vulnerabilities—these were the whispers of her soul, the evidence of a life lived authentically, a life that had been forged in the crucible of experience. In the quiet moments of self-reflection, she began to see the beauty in her imperfections, the intricate patterns of her scars, and the tapestry of her soul woven with threads of both light and shadow.

This newfound acceptance wasn't a sudden transformation, a flick of a switch. It was a gradual shift, a slow and steady dismantling of the walls she had erected around her heart. Each time she dared to be vulnerable, to shed a layer of her carefully constructed persona, she moved closer to the core of her being. She started to savor the moments of discomfort, recognizing them as opportunities for growth. The fear that had once held her captive began to lose its grip. The whispers of doubt were gradually drowned out by the burgeoning confidence that came from embracing her whole self.

The world, she realized, wasn't looking for a perfect woman; it was looking for a woman who was truly herself. And in the process of embracing her imperfections, Amelia found a strength she never knew she possessed. She realized that her worth was not tied to her ability to be perfect, but to her willingness to be authentically herself.

It was a liberating revelation, a gentle nudge towards a life lived in harmony with her true self. The journey towards self-acceptance was ongoing, a constant dance between embracing her flaws and celebrating the beauty that resided within them. It was a journey she would continue to walk with newfound confidence, a journey fueled by the liberating truth of her own imperfection.

Meaningful Relationships

Amelia had always been a good girl, a label she wore like a second skin. It had been her shield, her protector, and her prison. Now, she was starting to realize that the walls of her own construction were crumbling, revealing the woman she had kept hidden for so long. The journey to unbind her soul had been fraught with internal conflict, a dance between the societal expectations she had internalized and the wild, untamed desires that simmered beneath the surface. But, as she navigated this transformative path, she began to understand that true liberation wasn't about defying expectations, but about embracing the entirety of herself, the good and the bad, the light and the darkness. And in this pursuit, she found herself drawn to individuals who mirrored her journey, individuals who challenged her, supported her, and helped her to see herself more clearly.

One such individual was Maya, a free-spirited artist who lived life on her own terms. Maya's vibrant energy and unapologetic self-expression resonated with Amelia, offering a glimpse into a world where societal constraints were seen

As mere suggestions, not unyielding laws. Maya's studio, a kaleidoscope of colors and textures, became a sanctuary for Amelia, a place where she could shed her carefully crafted persona and explore her creative impulses. Maya saw Amelia's vulnerability, her fear, and her longing for liberation, and she met her with compassion and encouragement, reminding her that she was worthy of love and acceptance, even in her imperfections.

Another connection Amelia forged was with Sarah, a woman who had navigated her own journey of self-discovery, breaking free from the

shackles of a restrictive marriage and finding her voice in the world. Sarah's strength, her resilience, and her open heart resonated with Amelia, giving her hope that she, too, could break free from the confines of her own self-imposed limitations. Sarah's vulnerability, her willingness to share her struggles and triumphs, created a safe space for Amelia to confront her own fears and to find the courage to embrace her own authenticity.

These were just a few of the women who played a significant role in Amelia's journey. Each one, in her own unique way, helped Amelia to see herself more clearly, to understand that her worth was not defined by societal expectations, but by her own internal compass, her own desires, and her own unique brilliance. These connections were not just friendships, they were threads woven into the fabric of Amelia's transformation, threads of understanding, of acceptance, and of shared empowerment.

Beyond these individual connections, Amelia found solace and inspiration in a community of women who shared her values, her aspirations, and her desire to break free from the limitations of a patriarchal society. These women, united by their commitment to self-discovery and liberation, formed a collective force of change, a network of support that lifted each other up, celebrated each other's successes, and held space for each other's vulnerabilities. In this community, Amelia found a sense of belonging, a recognition that she was not alone in her journey, and that her voice, her experience, and her aspirations were valued and celebrated.

Through these meaningful connections, Amelia began to understand the power of self-love. She started to recognize that her worth was not contingent on external validation, but on her own ability to love and accept herself, flaws and all. She learned to celebrate her strengths, to acknowledge her weaknesses, and to approach her journey with compassion and understanding. She realized that her journey was not about becoming someone else, but about embracing the unique individual she was born to be.

As Amelia continued to unravel the layers of her own conditioning, she began to understand that her journey was not merely about her own liberation, but about contributing to a larger movement of change. She recognized that her voice, her story, and her experiences held the power to inspire others to embrace their own authenticity, to challenge the status quo, and to create a world where women were empowered to live lives that were true to themselves. And so, Amelia's journey became a testament to the power of connection, a beacon of hope for others who were seeking to break free from the confines of societal expectations and to embrace the boundless possibilities that lay within their own souls.

Learning from Others

Amelia found herself drawn to stories of resilience, to the women who had weathered storms and emerged stronger. In the quiet corners of coffee shops and bustling city streets, she overheard fragments of conversations, glimpses into lives that resonated with her own longing for liberation. She listened intently to the tales of women who had defied expectations, who had dared to break free from the confines of societal norms and forge their own paths.

There was the woman at the bookstore, her eyes alight with a mischievous twinkle as she shared stories of her wild travels, and a life spent exploring the world on her own terms. Her words painted vivid pictures of bustling markets, ancient ruins, and breathtaking landscapes, each place a testament to her adventurous spirit. Amelia felt a surge of admiration for her courage, her willingness to embrace the unknown, and her fierce independence.

Then there was the woman at the yoga studio, her voice calm and measured as she spoke of her journey through grief and healing. She had lost her husband unexpectedly, a devastating blow that had shaken her world to its core. Yet, she had found strength in the depths of her despair, rising from the ashes of her loss to rebuild her life and embrace a new path. Amelia felt a deep connection to her story, recognizing the shared vulnerability of navigating life's unexpected turns.

These encounters, these brief glimpses into the lives of other women, were like tiny sparks igniting a fire within Amelia. They reminded her that she was not alone in her struggle, that others had walked similar paths and emerged triumphant. Their stories became beacons of hope, illuminating the possibility of a life lived on her own terms.

One evening, while sitting at a bustling bar, Amelia found herself drawn to a group of women laughing boisterously around a table. They were a diverse mix, from different backgrounds and walks of life, yet they seemed united by a shared energy, a spirit of camaraderie and empowerment. Amelia hesitantly approached their table, drawn by the warmth radiating from their laughter and the sense of freedom swirling around them.

The women welcomed her warmly, their smiles disarming and their laughter infectious. As the conversation flowed, Amelia learned that they were part of a women's group, a safe space for women to connect, support one another, and explore their own identities. They shared stories of their struggles, their triumphs, and their dreams, creating a tapestry of shared experiences that resonated with Amelia's own journey.

The group became a haven for Amelia, a place where she could shed the weight of her past and explore her true self without judgment. She found solace in their shared stories, in their unwavering support, and in their celebration of individuality. They were her tribe, her chosen family, a group of women who understood her journey, who encouraged her to embrace her own unique expression, and who celebrated her every step towards liberation.

Through these connections, Amelia realized the power of community, the strength that comes from sharing experiences and supporting one another. She understood that she was not alone in her journey, that others had faced similar challenges and emerged stronger. She saw the resilience of women, their ability to overcome adversity, and their unwavering commitment to living authentically.

The stories of these women, their struggles and triumphs, became a source of inspiration for Amelia. They fueled her own journey of self-discovery, reminding her that she had the power to break free from the constraints of societal expectations and to embrace her own unique path. She was no longer bound by the limitations of her past or the expectations of others. She was free to explore, to experiment, to redefine herself, and to embrace the power of her own voice.

Building a Community

Amelia's newfound exploration of her desires and sexuality led her to seek out a community where she could be truly herself. It was during a weekend workshop on women's empowerment and sexuality that she first encountered a group of women who shared her values and aspirations. The workshop, hosted by a vibrant, outspoken woman named Maya, felt like a safe haven, a place where women could explore their desires, share their stories, and support each other without judgment.

It was a revelation for Amelia, a stark contrast to the conservative, judgmental environment she had been accustomed to. In this space, women openly discussed their experiences with pleasure, their struggles with societal expectations, and their journeys towards self-discovery. It was refreshing to be surrounded by women who spoke openly about their sexuality without shame or guilt, women who embraced their vulnerability and celebrated their differences.

Amelia found herself drawn to the shared energy of this community. There was a sense of collective strength and shared purpose, a recognition that they were all in this together, navigating the complexities of womanhood and challenging the limitations imposed by society. She felt seen and understood in a way she never had before.

The women in this community became her tribe, a network of support and encouragement as she continued to unravel the layers of her own identity. They shared their own stories of struggle and triumph, offering insights and advice that resonated deeply with Amelia's experience. They held space for her vulnerabilities, celebrating her growth and offering a listening ear when she needed it most.

Through shared experiences, workshops, and intimate gatherings, Amelia discovered the power of connection, the strength that comes from belonging to a community that truly understands and accepts you. She felt a sense of belonging that transcended geographical boundaries, a connection that went beyond surface-level friendships. This community provided a safe space for her to explore her desires, to express her fears, and to celebrate her triumphs, all without judgment.

The community also offered a sense of purpose, a shared mission to empower women and challenge societal norms. They organized events and workshops that aimed to educate and inspire, breaking down the walls of silence surrounding women's sexuality and self-discovery. Amelia found a sense of fulfillment in contributing to this mission, sharing her own story and inspiring others to embrace their own freedom.

The community was more than just a support system; it was a catalyst for growth and transformation. The women in this group encouraged Amelia to step out of her comfort zone, to challenge her own beliefs, and to embrace her authentic self. They reminded her that she was not alone, that there were countless women who had walked similar paths and emerged stronger and more empowered.

One particularly memorable event was a weekend retreat held in a secluded cabin nestled in the woods. Surrounded by nature and the company of like-minded women, Amelia felt a deep sense of peace and belonging. They spent the weekend engaged in various activities that encouraged self- reflection, creative expression, and connection. They shared their stories, vulnerabilities, and dreams, creating a space of mutual support and understanding.

During a circle activity where each woman was invited to share a personal truth, Amelia found herself revealing a painful childhood memory that had haunted her for years. The women listened with empathy and compassion, offering words of support and encouragement. It was in this space of vulnerability and shared understanding that Amelia finally began to release the shame and guilt that had been holding her back.

As the weekend drew to a close, Amelia felt a profound sense of gratitude for the community she had found. It wasn't just a group of women who shared similar interests; it was a family, a chosen tribe that supported her growth and celebrated her authenticity. This community became a vital part of Amelia's journey, providing her with the strength and resilience to navigate the challenges of self-discovery and embrace the freedom that comes with living authentically.

It was through this community that Amelia truly began to understand the power of connection, the strength that comes from being seen, understood, and supported by others. The community became a beacon of hope, a testament to the transformative power of shared experiences, and a reminder that we are all interconnected, united by our shared humanity and our journey towards self-discovery.

The Importance of Self-love

Amelia's journey was not just about breaking free from societal expectations, it was about reclaiming her power and finding her own truth. It was about understanding that her worth wasn't tied to her ability to conform but to her willingness to be authentically herself. This realization didn't come overnight; it was a slow, arduous process, a peeling back of layers, a constant battle against the internalized messages that had shaped her for so long.

As Amelia delved deeper into her journey, she began to understand that true freedom wasn't about doing whatever she wanted; it was about making choices that aligned with her values, her desires, and her authentic self. It was about listening to her inner voice, respecting her boundaries, and honoring her needs.

She started to cultivate a deep sense of self-love and compassion. She practiced self-care, taking time for herself to rest, recharge, and nurture her body, mind, and soul. She learned to be kind to herself, forgiving her mistakes and celebrating her victories.

Amelia began to notice a shift in her perspective. She no longer saw herself as flawed or inadequate. Instead, she embraced her imperfections, recognizing them as part of her unique tapestry. She learned to accept herself completely, flaws and all, because she understood that her worth was not contingent on her ability to be perfect.

This self-acceptance wasn't about ignoring her shortcomings or pretending they didn't exist. It was about choosing to see herself with compassion, understanding that she was a work in progress, and that she was worthy of love and acceptance regardless of her mistakes.

Amelia began to notice how her self-love radiated outwards, influencing her relationships with others. She found herself less willing to tolerate disrespect or mistreatment. She set boundaries, protecting her energy and prioritizing her well- being.

Her self-love wasn't just about her own happiness; it also allowed her to be more present and compassionate towards others. She found herself more empathetic, more understanding, and more willing to offer kindness and support.

This newfound self-love was the cornerstone of Amelia's journey. It gave her the strength to navigate the complexities of life, to confront her fears, and to embrace the unknown. It was a constant source of support, a guiding light that led her towards a life that was truly her own.

As Amelia continued to cultivate self-love, she discovered that it was not a destination but a lifelong journey. It was a practice, a commitment to nurturing her own well-being and honoring her authentic self. It was a choice she made every day, a reminder that she was worthy of love, acceptance, and happiness.

Finding Her Tribe

Amelia's journey of self-discovery wasn't just about internal exploration; it was about finding her place in the world. She realized that true liberation wasn't just about breaking free from societal expectations but also about building a community that celebrated her authentic self. This wasn't about conforming to a group; it was about finding her tribe, the people who saw her for who she truly was, the "bad girl" and the "good girl" interwoven.

Her quest began with a conscious effort to step out of her comfort zone. She started attending workshops and events that resonated with her newfound sense of self. At first, these gatherings were filled with a mix of anxiety and excitement. The fear of being judged or misunderstood was always present, but the desire to connect with like-minded individuals outweighed her apprehension.

One evening, Amelia found herself at a women's empowerment circle. The energy in the room was palpable, a blend of vulnerability and strength. As the women shared their stories, Amelia felt a sense of belonging she had never experienced before. There was no judgment, only understanding and acceptance. The women spoke of their struggles, their triumphs, and their desires, creating a safe space for vulnerability and authenticity. It was in this circle that Amelia began to shed the layers of self-doubt and societal conditioning.

She started meeting women who, like her, were breaking free from the shackles of tradition and societal norms. They were artists, entrepreneurs, activists, healers, and writers, each one a unique expression of female power. Amelia learned from their experiences, their wisdom, and their resilience. These women became her mentors, her confidantes, and her mirrors, reflecting back to her the strength and beauty she had long suppressed.

One particular woman, a seasoned artist named Maya, had a profound impact on Amelia's journey. Maya, with her vibrant spirit and unapologetic self-expression, became a catalyst for Amelia's own creative awakening. She taught Amelia to embrace her artistic side, to see the beauty in her imperfections, and to use her creativity as a form of self- expression.

Through these connections, Amelia realized that true liberation wasn't about erasing the "good girl" persona she had cultivated; it was about integrating both aspects of herself. The "bad girl" wasn't a separate entity; it was a part of her, a force that fueled her passion and her desire for self- expression.

Amelia discovered that her tribe wasn't just a group of women; it was a mosaic of individuals from diverse backgrounds, united by a shared desire for authenticity and connection. They celebrated her quirks, her vulnerabilities, and her unfiltered self. They encouraged her to pursue her passions, to embrace her sexuality, and to speak her truth without fear of judgment.

This newfound tribe provided Amelia with the support and encouragement she needed to navigate the complexities of her journey. They celebrated her successes and held her hand through her struggles. They became her anchors, reminding her of her strength, her resilience, and her inherent worth.

Amelia's journey wasn't a linear progression; it was a winding path filled with moments of doubt, fear, and self- discovery. But her tribe was always there, providing her with the love, support, and encouragement she needed to keep moving forward. They were the lighthouse in the storm, guiding her through the choppy waters of self-discovery, reminding her that she wasn't alone on her journey.

The power of connection, Amelia discovered, wasn't just about finding her tribe; it was about becoming a part of a collective force for change. Together, they would challenge societal norms, break free from limiting beliefs, and create a world where every woman could embrace her authentic self without fear of judgment or oppression.

A New Challenge

Amelia had built a life of resilience. She had confronted her past, healed old wounds, and reclaimed her voice. The woman who had once been shackled by fear and societal expectations had become a beacon of self-love and empowerment. But life, in its capricious nature, had a way of throwing curveballs, even to those who had learned to navigate its complexities with grace.

This new challenge arrived in the form of an unexpected betrayal. It wasn't a grand, dramatic act, but a subtle erosion of trust, a slow and insidious unraveling of a relationship Amelia had believed to be rock solid. It was the kind of betrayal that left her feeling foolish, questioning her judgment and her ability to discern genuine connection from superficial charm.

The realization struck her like a cold wave, washing away the warmth of her newfound confidence. The man she had believed to be her soul mate, the one who had promised unwavering support and unwavering love, had proven to be a mirage, a shimmering illusion in the desert of her trust. He had been unfaithful, not just physically but emotionally, investing his affections in someone else while continuing to cultivate the facade of their shared future.

The initial shock was followed by a wave of anger, a searing heat that threatened to consume her. How could someone she had trusted so deeply, someone who had sworn to love and cherish her, betray her in such a profound way? The anger morphed into a bitter cocktail of heartbreak and self-doubt, leaving her reeling in the aftermath of a shattered illusion.

Amelia had always prided herself on her strength, her ability to weather life's storms with grace and fortitude. But this betrayal, this shattering of her faith in love, felt different. It cut deeper, exposing a vulnerability she had believed she had conquered. She found herself retreating into a familiar

Pattern of self-blame, questioning her worthiness and replaying the events of the past, searching for clues that she had missed, for hints that she should have seen.

Yet, amidst the pain and the self-recrimination, a flicker of Amelia's former resilience began to ignite. This wasn't the first time she had faced heartbreak, but this time, she was armed with a newfound understanding of her own worth. She had learned to value her own needs and desires, to recognize the importance of boundaries and self-love. She knew that she deserved better than this, that she was worthy of a love that was genuine, unwavering, and reciprocal.

The familiar pull to revert back to her old patterns, to retreat into the safety of her shell, was strong. The fear of being hurt again, the fear of facing another disappointment, threatened to suffocate her burgeoning sense of self-worth. But Amelia had come too far, had endured too much to allow herself to be consumed by fear. She had tasted freedom, the exhilarating taste of authenticity and self-expression, and she wasn't willing to relinquish it for the comfort of a familiar cage.

This time, she refused to drown in self-pity. She refused to let this betrayal define her. Instead, she chose to channel her pain into fuel for her growth, a catalyst for further self- discovery. She recognized the strength she had cultivated, the resilience she had honed in the fires of past trials. She knew that this too, would pass, that the hurt would fade, and that she would emerge from this crucible even stronger than before.

The journey wasn't easy. There were moments of vulnerability, moments of doubt, moments when she felt like she was losing her footing. But she found solace in her newfound connection with herself, in her understanding of her own worth and the inherent power within her. She reached out to trusted friends and mentors, seeking solace and support, reminding herself that she was not alone in her pain.

She leaned into the lessons she had learned, drawing strength from her past triumphs. She reminded herself that the betrayal wasn't a reflection of her worth, but a testament to the flawed nature of the person who had chosen to hurt her. It was not a rejection of her, but a reflection of their own limitations.

Amelia began to see the betrayal as a catalyst for a deeper level of self-awareness, a challenge that forced her to confront her own fears and vulnerabilities. She embraced her imperfections, recognizing that they were not weaknesses but integral parts of what made her unique. She learned to trust her intuition, to listen to her own needs and desires, to prioritize her own well-being.

She sought solace in the beauty of the world around her, finding solace in nature's embrace, in the vibrant colors of a sunset, in the whispered secrets of the wind. She reconnected with her passions, finding joy in pursuing her interests, in expressing her creativity, in reminding herself of the vibrant spirit that resided within her.

The healing process wasn't linear. It was a winding path, with its own detours and unexpected turns. But Amelia persevered, drawing strength from her inner wellspring of resilience. She understood that the true measure of her strength wasn't in avoiding pain, but in her ability to rise above it, to learn from it, and to emerge from it even stronger.

She knew that the path to healing wouldn't be easy, but she also knew that she was ready to navigate it, ready to embrace the lessons it held, ready to emerge from this crucible a more authentic, more resilient version of herself. The betrayal had broken her heart, but it had also ignited a flame within her, a flame of self-love, self-acceptance, and a resolute determination to live a life that was true to her authentic self.

The Fear of Regression

The quiet hum of the city outside my window couldn't mask the cacophony of my own mind. I was back in that familiar, unwelcome space, a space I'd thought I'd escaped forever. The fear, the doubt, the whispering anxieties that had once clung to me like a shadow, were returning. They were a chorus of voices, chanting a refrain I knew all too well: "You'll never last. You'll go back to your old ways. This newfound freedom is just a phase."

The air felt thick with the weight of the past. My hands trembled, not from the chill of the evening air, but from the tremors of an internal earthquake. The world I'd so meticulously built, a world of carefully curated experiences, of restrained passions and contained emotions, seemed to be crumbling around me.

I was a woman on a tightrope, walking a path I'd never imagined for myself. The fear of falling was a constant companion, its icy grip tightening around my heart.

The freedom I'd fought so hard to claim, the one that allowed me to explore the depths of my desires, to embrace the "bad girl" I'd kept chained inside for so long, now felt like a fragile butterfly, its delicate wings threatened by the gust of my doubts.

What if I was wrong? What if this wasn't real, this sense of liberation, this newfound confidence? What if I was fooling myself, playing a role, a charade?

The familiar anxieties began to weave into my thoughts like tendrils of smoke slowly obscuring the light. I felt myself yearning for the safety of the old me, me who had mastered the art of conformity, of fitting into the neat little box society had created for me.

I was terrified of the thought of going back, of retreating to the safe haven of the familiar, of relinquishing the autonomy I'd fought so hard to claim. Yet, the whispers of doubt grew louder, their insidious rhythm drumming in my ears, a relentless beat that threatened to drown out the faint echoes of my newfound self.

Memories of my past self, the "good girl" I'd painstakingly crafted, flickered through my mind, a haunting reminder of who I was, who I had been forced to be. The memories were a tangled web of expectations, of societal norms, of the relentless pressure to conform, to silence my desires, to suppress my true self.

I had walked away from that world, from the confines of the "good girl" persona, but the echo of its voice still resonated within me. The chains may have been broken, but the scars of the past, the remnants of that life, still lingered.

I tried to push the doubts aside, to silence the voices of fear, but they persisted, a persistent echo of the past, a reminder of the life I'd left behind. I tried to find solace in the freedom

I'd found, to hold onto the strength I'd cultivated, but the fear was a relentless current, threatening to pull me back to the shore I'd so desperately escaped.

The world outside my window buzzed with life, a kaleidoscope of activity that seemed to mock my internal turmoil. I felt myself shrinking, retreating further into the shadows of my own mind.

It was as if the very air I breathed was thick with uncertainty, the world around me blurring as the familiar fear of regression tightened its grip.

The city lights twinkled like a distant constellation, a reminder of the vastness of the world beyond my window, a world I was so afraid to lose myself in.

I was a woman on a precipice, teetering on the edge of a self-inflicted chasm. One foot in the darkness of the past, the other tentatively reaching for the unknown future.

I knew, deep down, that the path ahead was uncertain, that there would be obstacles, challenges, and moments of doubt. But I also knew that I couldn't let the fear of regression dictate my path. I had to find a way to navigate the treacherous waters of my own mind, to silence the whispers of doubt and embrace the freedom I'd fought so hard to claim.

The fear was a constant companion, but I couldn't let it become my master. I had to find a way to move forward, to continue my journey, to embrace the unknown with the same courage I'd shown when I first dared to step out of the shadows.

I was a woman on a journey, and the road ahead was long and winding, but I knew that the journey was worth taking. The liberation I'd found, the woman I was becoming, was worth fighting for, even if it meant battling the ghosts of my own past.

I took a deep breath, the city lights shimmering like a beacon of hope in the darkness of my doubt. It was time to face the fear, to confront the whispering anxieties, and to hold onto the fragile butterfly of freedom, even if it meant letting go of the comfort of the familiar.

Learning from Setbacks

Amelia found herself at a crossroads. The exhilaration of her recent self-discovery had been abruptly interrupted by a painful setback. A business venture she had poured her heart and soul into had crumbled, leaving her feeling vulnerable and adrift. The echoes of the "good girl" she had fought so hard to shed resonated within her, whispering doubts and anxieties.

"What if I'm not strong enough?" The question echoed through her mind like a haunting melody. "What if all of this was just a fleeting illusion, a temporary rebellion that will inevitably be swallowed by the crushing weight of reality?"

The temptation to retreat to her old patterns, to seek solace in the familiar confines of societal expectations, was a powerful force. The world seemed to be pushing back, reminding her of the fragility of her newfound freedom.

But amidst the storm of self-doubt, a spark of resilience ignited within her. Amelia had faced challenges before, each one chipping away at the layers of self-imposed limitations. She had learned that the most profound growth often emerged from the ashes of adversity. Setbacks, she realized, were not failures but opportunities for reflection, re-evaluation, and a deeper understanding of her own strength.

She recalled the unwavering support of her newly found community – the women who had shared their own stories of resilience and triumph, reminding her that she was not alone in her struggles. Their words resonated in her heart, urging her to hold onto the belief that she possessed the inner fortitude to navigate this storm.

Instead of succumbing to the fear of regression, Amelia chose to embrace the challenge. She began to dissect the setback, seeking lessons instead of assigning blame. She examined her decisions, her strategies, and her vulnerabilities, accepting responsibility for her part in the outcome. The process was painful, but she refused to shy away from the discomfort.

She dug deep into her newly acquired tools of self- compassion and mindfulness, practicing gratitude for the lessons learned and the strength she had discovered. She allowed herself to grieve the loss of her dream while simultaneously celebrating the growth it had ignited.

As she processed the setback, Amelia began to notice a shift within her. The fear of regression had been replaced by a sense of resolve, a renewed commitment to her own liberation. The setback had not broken her but had instead forged a deeper understanding of her resilience. She realized that true freedom was not a static state but an ongoing journey, a path that inevitably included both triumphs and setbacks.

With a newfound clarity, Amelia began to reframe her perspective. She acknowledged the value of the lessons learned, recognizing that they were essential stepping stones on her path to self-discovery. She understood that growth often came in unexpected packages, disguised as setbacks, failures, and heartbreaks. The key, she realized, was to embrace the challenges, learn from them, and emerge stronger, more resilient, and more deeply connected to her own authentic self.

The setback had tested her limits, but it had also reminded her of her incredible capacity for growth, adaptation, and resilience. She had not simply survived the storm, but she had emerged stronger, more self-aware, and more deeply connected to the power within.

The unexpected turn in her journey had served as a catalyst for a deeper exploration of her own strength and resilience. Amelia had learned that the greatest challenges were not those that threatened to break her but those that forced her to dig deeper within, to uncover the depths of her courage and determination.

She knew that the path ahead would not be easy, that there would inevitably be more setbacks, more challenges, and more unexpected turns. But she also knew, with an unshakeable certainty, that she possessed the inner strength to face whatever came her way. She had learned to embrace the journey, to appreciate the lessons, and to trust in the power of her own resilience.

Amelia's journey was far from over. Her story was still unfolding, each chapter offering new lessons, unexpected turns, and opportunities for growth. But through it all, one thing remained constant – her unwavering commitment to her own liberation, her unwavering belief in her own strength, and her unwavering determination to live a life that was true to her authentic self.

The Power of Perseverance

The unexpected turn came in the form of a sudden job loss. The comfortable routine Amelia had built, the one she had believed was a sign of her success, crumbled in a matter of days. The fear that had always lurked beneath the surface, the fear of failing, of not meeting expectations, threatened to engulf her entirely. The "good girl" within whispered its familiar anxieties: "What will people think? How will you support yourself? You should have been more careful."

The "bad girl," however, had a different message. She whispered, "This is an opportunity, Amelia. You've been yearning for a change, for a chance to rewrite your story. This is your chance to break free, to choose a path that truly resonates with you."

Amelia, caught between these two voices, found herself at a crossroads. She could cling to the familiar, the safe, the expected, and try to rebuild what she had lost. Or she could embrace the unknown, the terrifying, the exhilarating, and forge a path that truly reflected her authentic self.

For the first time, the thought of rebuilding the same life, of conforming to the same expectations, felt suffocating. The fear of failure, the constant pressure to be perfect, felt like a heavy cloak she could no longer bear. She realized that true freedom, the freedom she had craved, wasn't about achieving a certain level of success, but about creating a life that felt truly aligned with her desires, her needs, and her own unique expression.

The journey had been challenging, filled with moments of self-doubt and fear, but it had also been exhilarating. Amelia had discovered a strength within herself that she never knew existed, a resilience that allowed her to face her fears and embrace the unknown. The "bad girl," once a whispered voice, now stood tall, a confident and unapologetic expression of her truest self.

This new challenge, however, tested her. The fear of regression, of losing the ground she had fought so hard to gain, threatened to consume her. She struggled to maintain the courage, the self-belief, and the sense of agency that had become her guiding principles. The temptation to return to the familiar patterns, to seek validation from external sources, felt like a siren song pulling her back into the comfortable cage of expectations.

But Amelia had learned a valuable lesson. She had learned that true freedom wasn't a destination, but an ongoing journey. It was about embracing the ebbs and flows of life, the highs and lows, the triumphs and setbacks. It was about learning from mistakes, picking herself up after falling, and continuing to move forward with courage and resilience.

This job loss was not a failure, but an opportunity. It was a chance to redefine her success, to rewrite her story, and to create a life that was truly her own. It was a reminder that she had the power to choose her own path, to define her own worth, and to embrace the unpredictable nature of life with an open heart and a determined spirit.

So, Amelia, armed with the lessons she had learned, faced the challenge head-on. She leaned into the fear, acknowledging its presence without allowing it to paralyze her. She remembered the power she had found within herself, the resilience she had cultivated, and the unwavering belief in her own ability to navigate this new terrain.

She began to explore new possibilities, to embrace opportunities that aligned with her passions and her authentic self. She sought out support systems that encouraged her growth and celebrated her individuality. She confronted the internal voices of doubt with affirmations of self-worth and self-love.

Slowly, with each step, she rediscovered her strength. She realized that the power she had found was not a temporary state, but a wellspring of resilience that she could tap into whenever she needed it. She understood that the "bad girl" was not a separate entity, but an integral part of her being, a force that empowered her to break free from the constraints of societal expectations and to claim her rightful place in the world.

As she navigated the uncertainties of this unexpected turn, Amelia discovered a new level of strength within herself. She learned that true freedom wasn't about avoiding challenges, but about facing them head-on, with courage, resilience, and a deep sense of self-belief. She understood that setbacks were not failures, but opportunities for growth, for redefining success, and for creating a life that was truly her own.

The unexpected turn had not shattered her, but had instead served as a catalyst for further growth and self-discovery. It had awakened a new level of determination within her, a sense of purpose that was fueled by the realization that she had the power to shape her own destiny, to rewrite her own story, and to create a life that reflected her truest self. And that, she realized, was the most profound freedom of all.

Emerging Stronger

The unexpected challenge had been a whirlwind of emotions, a test of Amelia's newfound strength and resilience. It had felt like a betrayal, a cruel twist of fate that threatened to unravel all the progress she had made. She'd found herself questioning everything she'd believed in, her ability to maintain her newfound freedom, and even her own sanity. The urge to retreat, to hide within the familiar confines of her old self, was almost overwhelming. The fear of regression, of slipping back into the cage of expectations, was a palpable presence, a constant reminder of the vulnerability she'd exposed.

But this time, something felt different. The fear was still there, but it was countered by a new and powerful force—an unwavering determination to persevere. The lessons she had learned through her journey, the countless hours spent unraveling the layers of societal conditioning, and the unwavering support of her newfound community had left an indelible mark on her soul.

The challenge, however, had not been a simple test of her will. It had forced Amelia to confront the deepest shadows within her, the remnants of past trauma that had long been buried under layers of denial and self-deception. The pain she'd felt, the sense of betrayal and disillusionment, had triggered a deep-seated fear of abandonment, a fear she'd carried since childhood.

It was in the depths of this darkness, facing the raw vulnerability of her past, that Amelia discovered a profound strength she had never known she possessed. She had allowed herself to break down, to surrender to the pain and the fear, acknowledging it instead of trying to suppress it. In that moment of vulnerability, she found the courage to face her demons head-on, to confront the source of her fear and the root of her insecurities.

This process of facing her demons had been agonizing, a journey through the darkest corners of her soul. Yet, through this journey, Amelia found an unexpected source of power— the power of self-compassion. She understood that her past experiences, however painful, did not define her. She had learned to forgive herself, to release the burden of shame and guilt that had weighed her down for so long. This act of self- forgiveness was the key to unlocking a new level of self- acceptance, a deeper understanding of her own resilience, and a profound sense of freedom.

Emerging from the challenge, Amelia felt a shift within her. The world seemed brighter, clearer, and filled with a renewed sense of possibility. She had faced her demons, healed the wounds of her past, and emerged stronger, more confident, and more deeply connected to her authentic self. The experience had been a crucible, a transformative fire that had burned away the layers of fear, insecurity, and self- doubt, leaving behind a core of strength and unwavering self-belief.

Her journey had been far from easy. There had been moments of doubt, moments of despair, and moments when she'd felt utterly lost. But

through it all, she had learned to trust her own intuition, to listen to the whispers of her own heart, and to embrace the power of her own agency. She had discovered that true freedom was not about achieving perfection, but about accepting herself wholeheartedly, flaws and all. It was about embracing the beauty of her imperfections, celebrating her uniqueness, and living a life that was true to her core values.

This newfound sense of freedom extended beyond her own personal journey. Amelia had learned that she had a responsibility to use her voice, her experiences, and her platform to inspire others to break free from the limitations of societal expectations and to embrace their own journeys of self-discovery. She understood that every woman, every individual, had the power to challenge the status quo, to create a more inclusive and equitable world, and to live a life that was authentically their own.

The unexpected turn had been a defining moment in Amelia's journey. It had been a crucible that had tested her resilience, forced her to confront her deepest fears, and ultimately led her to a deeper understanding of her own strength and the power of self-love. Emerging from the challenge, Amelia felt a profound sense of gratitude for the lessons she had learned, for the support she had received, and for the woman she had become. She knew that the journey was far from over, but she was ready to embrace the future, armed with the courage, resilience, and self-belief to face whatever came her way. The world was her oyster, and she was determined to make the most of every opportunity, to live a life that was truly her own, and to inspire others to do the same.

Reconciling with Family

The drive back to her parents' house was a symphony of conflicting emotions. A sense of liberation buzzed through her veins, the echo of the sun-warmed sand still clinging to her skin. But beneath that joyous hum, a low, throbbing unease pulsed. She knew the weight of her past, the carefully constructed image of the good girl, awaited her at the front door.

It had been months since Amelia had last visited. Months of her own exploration, a journey of shedding the old skin and embracing the woman she was becoming. The woman who craved adventure, who danced with reckless abandon, who relished the raw honesty of her desires. The woman who was still learning to love the complex tapestry of her being, flaws and all.

As she pulled into the familiar driveway, the pristine lawn and the manicured rose bushes that her mother meticulously tended seemed to mock her newfound freedom. Her stomach churned with a familiar cocktail of guilt and apprehension. She knew her parents would be delighted to see her, but the sheer joy of the reunion would be clouded by a subtle undercurrent of disappointment.

Amelia had always been the dutiful daughter, the one who followed the path laid out for her. The perfect child, the epitome of their religious values, a testament to their upbringing. The thought of their reaction, the whispers of disapproval that would inevitably follow, was a heavy cloak she felt draped across her shoulders.

It wasn't that her parents were deliberately cruel. They loved her deeply, and their intentions were always good. But their love was laced with expectations, a suffocating web of societal norms and religious beliefs that Amelia had once believed were unshakable. She had always known the whispers of "what will people think," the unspoken fear of her actions creating ripples of judgment and disapproval, were a silent force guiding her every move.

Opening the car door, she felt a familiar prickling on her skin, a sense of being watched, of being judged. As she entered the house, the familiar scent of lavender and freshly baked cookies filled her senses, a comforting but ultimately stifling aroma. Her mother greeted her with a wide, beaming smile, and her father followed closely behind, his embrace laced with the warmth of unconditional love.

But Amelia saw past the façade. The subtle tightening of her mother's lips, the way her father's eyes lingered on her attire, a departure from her usual conservative attire. Their love, though genuine, was tinged with a silent plea, a desperate wish for her to stay within the confines of the life they had envisioned for her.

Amelia had been so careful, so deliberate in her transformation. She hadn't made any dramatic changes, choosing to introduce her newfound self gradually, like a flower cautiously opening its petals to the sun. But as the days passed, she felt the weight of their expectations pressing down on her, a constant reminder of the life she had left behind.

One evening, her mother cornered her in the kitchen, her eyes filled with concern. "Amelia, honey, are you sure you're happy with…well, with everything?" Her voice was laced with a hint of worry.

Amelia had expected this conversation. She had anticipated the probing questions, the veiled criticisms that would inevitably come. But she had learned to navigate these conversations with newfound strength. She met her mother's gaze with a quiet confidence. "Mother, I am happy. I am exploring, learning, and growing. I am becoming the woman I am meant to be."

Her mother's gaze softened, a glimmer of understanding flickering in her eyes. But the disappointment was still there, an unspoken plea for her daughter to return to the familiar shores of their shared beliefs.

That night, Amelia lay awake in her childhood room, the familiar scent of lavender and the faint echoes of her parents' prayers a reminder of the life she had left behind. The weight of their expectations, the unspoken disapproval, felt like a heavy stone in her chest.

And then, a strange thing happened. The familiar feelings of guilt and fear were replaced by a sense of calm acceptance. She had come so far, pushing past the boundaries of her comfort zone, confronting the demons of her past. And though she still carried the scars of her upbringing, the scars of societal expectations, she had finally learned to own her story. She had found the courage to be true to herself, and that, she realized, was a power she could never relinquish.

The next morning, Amelia approached her parents, a newfound sense of peace radiating from her. She spoke with honesty and compassion, acknowledging their love and their concerns. She explained her need for freedom, her desire to explore, to learn, to embrace the woman she was becoming.

Their reaction was not the one she had expected. Their eyes filled with tears, not of anger or disappointment, but of a deep and abiding love. Their voices, though laced with a touch of sadness, were filled with acceptance. They understood that their daughter had grown, that she had embarked on a journey of self-discovery, and that they, though hesitant, would support her along the way.

The weight of the past still lingered, but it had shifted. It was no longer a suffocating burden but a reminder of her journey, a testament to her resilience. She knew that reconciling with her family would be an ongoing process, a journey of understanding and acceptance. But she had finally learned to walk with that weight, to carry it with grace and to find strength in the love she shared with those who had nurtured her, even as she ventured into the unknown.

Forgiveness and Acceptance

The air hung heavy with the scent of pine needles and the familiar aroma of baking bread wafting from the kitchen. It was Sunday, and the world outside our small-town church seemed to stand still, caught in the hushed reverence of the Sabbath. Yet, inside me, a storm raged. The sermon that morning had been about forgiveness, about letting go of anger and bitterness. It was a message I desperately needed to hear, but it also felt like a stark accusation aimed directly at me. For years, I had held onto a bitter cocktail of resentment and hurt, a toxic brew concocted from the past.

My childhood had been a tapestry woven with threads of love and strict religious teachings. My parents had meant well, their intentions pure, but their fervent faith had inadvertently painted a world where joy was often tinged with fear, and self-expression was a tightly controlled art form. I had been the "good girl," the embodiment of their hopes and dreams, the perfect daughter. But beneath that facade, a rebellious spirit simmered, yearning to break free from the confines of societal expectations. My adolescence was a time of silent rebellion, a period of pushing boundaries and testing limits, culminating in a decision that sent shockwaves through our family.

I had fallen in love, a love that burned with an intensity that both terrified and enthralled me. It was a love that defied the rules, the love that our small-town community deemed unsuitable, a love that dared to question the very foundations of our faith. My parents were heartbroken, their trust shattered. Their anger was a palpable force, their disappointment a crushing weight. I had betrayed their hopes, their ideals, and in their eyes, my soul. The pain of that betrayal had lingered, a heavy burden I carried with me, even years after the storm had passed.

But it was during that sermon, under the watchful gaze of stained-glass angels, that a realization dawned. Forgiveness wasn't about condoning the hurtful actions of others. It wasn't about overlooking the pain or dismissing the injustice. It was about releasing myself from the chains of anger, the shackles of resentment. It was about reclaiming my own peace, my own freedom.

I began to see that my parents, despite their actions, had also been victims of their own beliefs, prisoners of a rigid worldview that had left them afraid of the unknown. They had been taught that my rebellion was a sign of weakness, a transgression against God. Their fear had fueled their anger, their disappointment had become a weapon. But they were not monsters, they were flawed human beings, grappling with their own struggles.

The realization hit me like a wave, washing away the bitterness that had clung to me for so long. Forgiving them, however, was a slow process, a journey of gentle steps and internal negotiations. It meant acknowledging the hurt, owning my own anger, and then slowly releasing it, piece by piece. It meant forgiving myself for the choices I had made, for the pain I had inflicted, and for the years I had wasted trapped in the shadows of regret.

My journey of forgiveness was a long one, a winding path of introspection and self-discovery. It was a journey that led me to a place of profound acceptance, a place where I could finally see the complexity of my own story and the stories of those around me. It meant understanding that forgiveness wasn't a sign of weakness, but a testament to my own strength, my own resilience. It was a gift I gave myself, a gift of freedom.

As I walked out of the church that day, the world seemed brighter, the air lighter. The storm within me had subsided, leaving behind a fragile peace, a sense of release. The weight of the past, once a burden that threatened to crush me, was now a reminder of my journey, a testament to my strength. It was a reminder that forgiveness, even in the face of deep hurt, was not only possible but essential. It was the key to unlocking my own soul, freeing it from the chains of bitterness and allowing it to finally soar.

Setting Boundaries with Family

Amelia's heart pounded in her chest as she sat across from her parents at their kitchen table. It was the first time they'd all sat down together since she'd moved out, since she'd started living a life that was wholly her own, a life that defied the expectations they'd held for her since she was a child.

"I'm not sure what you're trying to say, Amelia," her mother said, her voice a low tremor. "It's just... a lot to take in. All of this. It's like you've become a stranger."

Amelia took a deep breath, her hand resting on the worn oak table. "Mom, I know it's been difficult, but I need you to understand. I'm not the same person I was when I was living at home. I've changed. I've grown."

Her father cleared his throat, his eyes filled with a mix of confusion and hurt. "But you're still our daughter. And we always want what's best for you."

"I know, Dad. And that's exactly what I'm doing. I'm living my life the way I want to live it, the way that feels true to me."

"What about your faith? You've always been a good girl, a devout Christian. What about all the teachings you've been raised with?"

Amelia felt a surge of frustration, but she took another deep breath, reminding herself that this was not about fighting. This was about communication, about setting boundaries, about protecting her own space.

"My faith is still important to me, Dad," she said, her voice calm and measured. "But it doesn't mean I have to live my life according to the expectations of others. I have my own beliefs and values, and I'm learning to live by them."

Her mother's eyes widened, her face etched with disapproval. "Are you saying you don't agree with what we've taught you?"

Amelia met her gaze directly. "Mom, I'm not saying I don't agree with everything you've taught me. I'm saying I'm learning to discern what resonates with me and what doesn't. I'm learning to listen to my own intuition, to my own heart."

The silence that followed was thick and heavy, filled with unspoken emotions. Amelia knew they were struggling to understand, to accept the new person she'd become. But she also knew that she had to be true to herself, even if it meant pushing back against the familiar and the comfortable.

"I need you to respect my choices," Amelia continued, her voice gaining strength. "I need you to understand that I'm not going to change just because you want me to. I'm not going to live my life according to your expectations anymore. I'm going to live it for me."

"Amelia, we just want you to be happy," her mother said, her voice filled with a desperate plea.

"I am happy," Amelia countered, her voice firm but gentle. "But my happiness doesn't depend on your approval. It depends on me being true to myself, on me living a life that is authentic to my soul."

Her parents looked at each other, a mix of sadness and confusion clouding their faces. Amelia felt a pang of empathy for them, for the hurt they were feeling. She knew this wasn't easy for them to accept, but she also knew that she couldn't sacrifice her own well-being for their comfort.

"It's not about being good or bad," Amelia added, her voice softening. "It's about finding your own path, about embracing your own truth. And that's what I'm doing."

"But what if you're wrong?" her mother asked, her voice trembling.

Amelia smiled, a flicker of warmth breaking through the tension. "Mom, even if I am wrong, I'd rather be wrong on my own terms than right on someone else's."

The weight of the conversation settled on the table between them, a tangible presence that spoke volumes about the complexities of family, of change, and of the journey to find oneself. It was a conversation that would continue, a dialogue that would be tested and challenged, but it was a dialogue that needed to happen.

For Amelia, it was a step towards finding her voice, towards reclaiming her autonomy, towards living a life that was truly her own. She knew it wouldn't be easy, but she was determined to forge her own path, to walk her own journey, even if it meant leaving behind the familiar and venturing into the unknown. For in that unknown, she had discovered a power that transcended the expectations and limitations of the past.

The Power of Letting Go

The crisp air of the mountaintop carried a sense of lightness, a stark contrast to the heaviness I had been carrying for so long. The past year had been a whirlwind of self-discovery, a journey that had forced me to confront the ghosts of my past, to acknowledge the patterns I had inherited, and to finally break free from their hold.

As I stood there, gazing at the vast expanse of the valley below, I realized that a significant shift had occurred within me. The anger I had harbored for years, the resentment I had carried towards my family, and the need to constantly control situations and people, were slowly starting to dissipate.

The path to forgiveness and acceptance had been arduous, filled with moments of doubt and fear. The years of conditioning, the ingrained messages about what a "good girl" should be, the expectations placed on me by a family rooted in tradition, had left their mark. I had spent so much energy trying to live up to these ideals, striving for their approval, which I had lost sight of who I truly was.

My journey had led me to a realization that the true weight of the past wasn't just about the events themselves, but about the narrative I had constructed around them. I had clung to the hurt, the anger, the sense of betrayal, believing that holding onto those emotions was a testament to my strength, a way of proving to myself that I was worthy of love and respect. But in reality, those emotions were keeping me trapped in a prison of my own making.

The turning point came when I realized that the need to control, to dictate, to change others was not a sign of strength, but of fear. The fear of vulnerability, the fear of being hurt again, the fear of being disappointed. But I had to understand that the control I exerted was not about protecting myself, it was about controlling the world around me to make it conform to my own expectations.

As I stood there on the mountaintop, I felt a wave of peace wash over me. It was a realization that true freedom was not about changing the world around me, but about accepting it for what it was. It was about letting go of the need to control, to mold, to manipulate, to make things fit my preconceived notions. It was about understanding that I couldn't change the past, but I could choose how it affected my present and my future.

Forgiveness, I realized, was not about condoning the past, but about releasing myself from the chains of resentment and anger. It was about choosing to move forward, to heal, and to embrace the present moment with an open heart and a clear mind. It was about understanding that the pain of the past could become a catalyst for growth and transformation.

I thought of my family, the people who had instilled these values in me, and the people I had loved and resented in equal measure. I saw them not as villains but as products of their own upbringing, their own conditioning, and their own fears. I saw them as flawed individuals, just like me, struggling to find their way in a world that often felt chaotic and unpredictable.

I realized that my journey wasn't about punishing them for their actions, but about forgiving them for their limitations, for their inability to understand the person I was becoming. It was about understanding that they had loved me in the only way they knew how, and that their love, though sometimes misguided, had been genuine.

Letting go didn't erase the hurt, the anger, the resentment. But it allowed me to reclaim my own power, to choose to live a life free from the shackles of the past. It was a choice to embrace the present moment, to acknowledge the beauty and the pain, the joy and the sorrow, and to find peace in the ebb and flow of life.

The air grew colder as the sun began its descent, painting the sky in hues of orange and pink. I took a deep breath, feeling a sense of lightness and freedom I had never known before. The past was still there, a part of my story, but it no longer held me captive. I was free. And for the first time in my life, I felt truly free.

Finding Peace with Her Roots

The car hummed along the winding road, the sun setting in a blaze of orange and pink, casting long shadows across the rolling hills. Amelia watched the landscape shift and change, her mind drifting back to the past, to the small town where she had grown up, to the strict religious upbringing that had shaped her beliefs, her morals, and her very identity. It was a world of black and white, of right and wrong, a world where her desires, her dreams, her very essence were often relegated to the shadows.

As she drove, a sense of peace settled over her. The tension that had always been a constant companion, the fear of judgment and disapproval, began to melt away. She had been on a journey of self-discovery, a tumultuous journey filled with challenges and triumphs, a journey that had led her to this place, this moment, where she could finally embrace the past without letting it define her.

The town of her childhood felt like a distant dream, a place she had outgrown, a place she had shed like an old, ill-fitting coat. The memories, however, were still there, etched in the crevices of her mind, a tapestry woven with love and tradition, but also with unspoken rules and suffocating expectations. The weight of her family's legacy, the whispered secrets and unspoken truths, had always pressed down on her, a burden she had carried for so long.

But now, as she looked out at the landscape, she realized that her past was not a prison but a stepping stone. It had taught her valuable lessons, instilled in her a strong sense of compassion and empathy, but it had also confined her, held her back from truly embracing her own desires, her own truth.

Amelia had confronted those shadows, those unspoken fears and insecurities, had faced the internal conflict that had raged within her, and had come out on the other side, stronger, more resilient, more authentic. She had learned to forgive her family, not for their actions, but for her own inability to break free from their expectations, to find her own voice, to define her own path.

She had also learned to forgive herself, to acknowledge her own complicity in the limitations she had imposed upon herself, the fear she had clung to, the dreams she had suppressed. The journey had been a long and winding one, filled with moments of doubt and fear, but it had also been a journey of self-discovery, of liberation, of reclaiming her own agency.

She was no longer the girl who had been raised in the shadow of a strict religious upbringing, the girl who had internalized the message that her worth was tied to her obedience and conformity. She was a woman who had found her voice, embraced her desires, and forged her own path. She had learned to love herself, flaws and all, to celebrate her individuality, to embrace the beauty of her imperfections.

The road stretched ahead, a path paved with the possibilities of a life lived on her own terms. She was no longer bound by the expectations of others, the rules of a world that had sought to confine her. She was free, unbound, her spirit soaring, her soul alight.

As the sun dipped below the horizon, painting the sky in hues of gold and crimson, Amelia felt a deep sense of gratitude, a quiet contentment that settled in her heart. She had come a long way, had faced her demons, had embraced her darkness, and had emerged into the light. She had found peace with her roots, acknowledging their influence while recognizing that she was no longer defined by them. She was a woman of her own making, a woman who had found her true self, a woman who had finally found peace.

Living Authentically

Amelia walked with a lightness in her step, a confidence she hadn't known before. The world felt different, alive with possibility. She no longer saw herself as a prisoner of expectations, a mere reflection of what society deemed acceptable. She was a kaleidoscope, a symphony of colors and emotions, a being with a heart that beat to its own rhythm. The world was a canvas upon which she painted her story, bold strokes of individuality defying the boundaries of conformity.

Her career was no longer a means to an end, but a platform for her voice. Amelia chose a path that resonated with her passions, one that allowed her to express her creativity and contribute to a world she believed in. She surrounded herself with people who embraced her uniqueness, those who saw her not for what she presented but for who she truly was.

Her wardrobe was a reflection of her liberated spirit. She wore colors that spoke to her soul, clothes that felt comfortable and empowering, a celebration of her body and its beauty. Gone were the days of hiding behind the shadows of conformity, replaced by a radiant expression of self-love.

Her relationships were built on honesty and authenticity. She chose partners who shared her desire for growth, who celebrated her flaws as much as her strengths. There was a vulnerability in her that emanated from a deep understanding of her worth, a knowing that she was deserving of love and respect.

Amelia's nights were no longer filled with the emptiness of societal expectations. Instead, they were filled with the vibrant energy of self-expression. She danced to the beat of her own heart, explored her desires with curiosity and freedom, and found pleasure in the simple act of being alive. Her sexuality was no longer a source of shame but a celebration of her sensuality, a testament to her power and her right to experience the world in all its richness.

Life wasn't always easy. There were days when the whispers of doubt crept back, reminding her of the societal expectations she had once internalized. But Amelia had learned to navigate these moments with a newfound resilience. She knew that her journey was a lifelong process, one that required courage, self-compassion, and an unwavering commitment to her truth.

Amelia had found her voice. She spoke her truth with confidence, not to seek validation from the outside world, but to honor the powerful being she had become. She shared her story, not to boast or seek praise, but to empower others to find their own liberation. She was a testament to the strength and beauty of the unbound soul, a living example of what it meant to live a life true to oneself.

Amelia had embraced her imperfections. She understood that her worth wasn't tied to her ability to conform or to achieve societal expectations. Her scars were badges of honor, reminders of the battles she had fought and won. Her vulnerability was a source of strength, a testament to her capacity for love and connection. She was a mosaic, a tapestry of experiences woven together to form the intricate masterpiece that was her.

Amelia's journey was a beacon of hope. It was a reminder that freedom wasn't a destination, but a continuous journey of growth and self-discovery. It was an invitation to shed the shackles of societal expectations and to embrace the beauty of being uniquely oneself. It was a call to action, a whisper of possibility, urging others to break free from the cage of conformity and to embrace the boundless potential of their own unbound soul.

The Beauty of Imperfection

The bathroom mirror was my canvas, and I was finally ready to paint a masterpiece. It wasn't about perfection; it was about authenticity. No longer would I try to erase the stretch marks that told the story of my body's journey. The faint scar on my cheek, a souvenir from a childhood mishap, was a reminder of my resilience, a testament to the fact that I had survived and thrived. The freckles that danced across my nose, a gift from my Irish ancestry, were badges of honor, evidence of my heritage and the sun's warm embrace. My imperfections were not flaws to be hidden, but rather, the very threads that wove the tapestry of my unique existence.

I had spent so many years striving for an unattainable ideal, a vision of beauty dictated by society's fickle standards. I had scrutinized my reflection, searching for flaws and imperfections, convinced that my worth was tied to my ability to fit into a mold that wasn't even mine. But in the depths of my soul, a quiet voice had been whispering, urging me to embrace the fullness of who I was.

My body, with its curves and bumps and scars, was my temple, a vessel for the spirit that resided within. It had carried me through countless adventures, endured heartbreak and joy, and served as a constant companion on my life's journey. It was time to honor its resilience, its strength, and its beauty, flaws and all.

As I gazed at my reflection, I saw not just a woman with imperfections, but a woman who was whole, complete, and perfectly imperfect. In the depths of my eyes, I saw the echoes of a life lived, the whispers of dreams fulfilled and the fire of dreams yet to be realized. I saw a woman who had emerged from the chrysalis of societal expectations, shedding the weight of those limiting beliefs and embracing the freedom to be her true self.

The beauty I saw was not confined to a symmetrical face or a flawless physique. It resided in the depth of my soul, in the vulnerability I embraced, in the authenticity I allowed to shine through. It was the beauty of a woman who had learned to love herself unconditionally, flaws and all, a woman who understood that true beauty lay not in conforming to external standards, but in embracing the unique essence of her being.

This realization was not just a fleeting epiphany; it was a profound shift in my understanding of beauty and self-worth. It was a liberation from the tyranny of societal expectations, a reclaiming of my body and my soul. I no longer needed to seek validation from the outside world; I had found it within myself. And in that moment, I felt a deep sense of peace, a quiet joy that emanated from the very core of my being.

This was the beauty of imperfection, the radiance of authenticity. This was the reclaimed self, a woman who had found her true voice and learned to celebrate the symphony of her own unique existence. And as I stepped out of the bathroom, I carried this newfound confidence with me, ready to face the world with an open heart, a fearless spirit, and a love for the flawed, beautiful woman that I was.

**Finding Her Voice

Amelia's voice, once a hushed whisper, began to rise. It started in small, quiet spaces, with her closest friends, where vulnerability felt safe and acceptance was guaranteed. She spoke about her desires, her frustrations, her fears, and the weight of the expectations she had carried for so long. The words tumbled out, raw and honest, like a long-dammed river finally finding its course.

Her friends, who had always known her as the "good girl," were surprised, but their surprise morphed into admiration. They saw in her a newfound strength, a boldness they had never witnessed before. She was no longer the girl who tiptoed around, afraid to ruffle feathers or speak her mind. She was a woman with a voice, and she was using it.

Amelia started to challenge the societal norms she had always accepted. She questioned the double standards, the expectations placed on women, and the limitations imposed by tradition. She spoke out against the injustices she had observed, the unspoken rules that held women back, and the assumptions that stifled their dreams.

Her voice wasn't always met with applause. There were those who bristled at her defiance, those who dismissed her opinions as radical or unreasonable. There were moments when her words were met with anger, dismissal, or even hostility. But Amelia learned to navigate these challenges with grace and conviction. She learned to stand her ground, to speak her truth even when it was uncomfortable, to defend her beliefs with unwavering determination.

Her voice began to reach beyond her immediate circle. She found a platform on social media, where she shared her experiences and her thoughts on feminism, sexuality, and self-discovery. She connected with other women who resonated with her story, who shared her struggles, and who sought the same freedom she had found.

Through her writing and her online presence, Amelia became a voice for the voiceless. She challenged the stereotypes that defined women, the expectations that limited their potential, and the pressures that made them feel inadequate. She spoke about the importance of self-love, the power of female connection, and the right to define one's own happiness. She encouraged other women to embrace their authenticity, to celebrate their differences, and to find their own voices.

Amelia's voice became a beacon of hope for women who felt lost, unheard, and unseen. It was a reminder that they weren't alone, that their experiences mattered, and that they had the power to create the lives they desired. She was living proof that it was possible to break free from the constraints of societal expectations and to live authentically, fully, and with purpose.

Amelia's journey was far from over. She continued to face challenges, to grapple with her own insecurities, and to question her own beliefs. But she had learned that her voice was her greatest asset, her most powerful tool. She knew that it could be a force for change, a catalyst for healing, and a source of empowerment for herself and others. Amelia's voice was not just a means of communication; it was a symbol of liberation, a testament to the resilience of the human spirit, and a beacon of hope for a future where women were free to be their true selves.

A Life of Purpose

Amelia's life took on a vibrant tapestry of meaning and purpose. She had embraced her authentic self, shedding the constricting layers of societal expectations and the internalized guilt that had once weighed her down. She discovered a potent sense of liberation, a freedom to be her most genuine self, without fear of judgment or the suffocating need to conform.

This newfound freedom was a beacon, guiding her actions and shaping her choices. She understood that her life was not just a series of events or accomplishments but a canvas on which she could paint her own unique masterpiece. The strokes were her choices, her actions, and her unwavering commitment to living a life that aligned with her values and beliefs.

Her passion for social justice had awakened, driven by a burning desire to create a more equitable and compassionate world. Amelia channeled her energy into various projects, volunteering with organizations that supported marginalized communities and advocating for policies that promoted social equality. Her voice, once timid and hesitant, now resonated with conviction and purpose, inspiring others to join her in the pursuit of a more just world.

Her creative spirit blossomed as she expressed herself through art, writing, and music. She found solace and joy in crafting stories that touched the hearts and minds of others, sharing her experiences and insights in a way that connected her to a wider community. Her art became a conduit for her emotions, a powerful form of communication that transcended words.

Amelia's journey of self-discovery had led her to a deep understanding of the power of connection. She cultivated meaningful relationships, surrounding herself with individuals who supported her growth and embraced her authentic self. These relationships were not just casual acquaintances; they were bonds built on trust, mutual respect, and a shared vision of a world where everyone felt empowered to be their true selves.

She recognized the profound impact of her choices on the world around her. She understood that her actions had a ripple effect, influencing not only her own life but the lives of those she interacted with. This realization fueled her commitment to making a positive impact on the world, starting with small acts of kindness and generosity that extended outwards, touching the lives of others in unexpected ways.

Amelia's life became a testament to the transformative power of self-discovery. She had faced her fears, embraced her desires, and ultimately found her purpose. Her story was not just her own, but a beacon of hope and inspiration for others who were seeking their own path to freedom and fulfillment. She had proven that living authentically, embracing one's true self, and making a positive impact on the world was not just a dream but a tangible reality. Amelia's journey was a testament to the resilience of the human spirit, a reminder that each of us has the power to create a life that is both fulfilling and meaningful.

The Unbound Soul

The crisp autumn air nipped at Amelia's cheeks as she stood on the precipice of a mountain overlooking a valley painted in shades of amber and gold. Below, the world stretched out before her, vast and alive, mirroring the boundless possibilities that now resonated within her. This moment, perched atop the mountain, felt like the culmination of a long, arduous journey, a journey that had taken her from the confines of societal expectations to the uncharted territories of her own soul.

Her heart thrummed with a quiet, deep joy, a sensation so profound it felt like a homecoming. It wasn't just the breathtaking panorama before her that filled her with such profound contentment, but the realization that she had finally arrived at a place of true self-acceptance. The shackles of guilt, shame, and societal pressure that had once bound her had finally fallen away, revealing a woman who was bold, vibrant, and free.

This wasn't a sudden metamorphosis; it had been a gradual unfolding, a process of peeling away layers of conditioning and embracing the raw, unfiltered essence of who she was. There had been times when doubt had threatened to engulf her, when the whispers of insecurity had threatened to drag her back to the familiar confines of her old life. But with each challenge, each hurdle she overcame, her resolve had solidified, her spirit ignited with a fiery determination to live authentically.

The journey had been fraught with moments of vulnerability, times when she had been forced to confront the shadows of her past, to grapple with the scars that societal expectations had etched upon her soul. But with each confrontation, she had emerged stronger, her spirit tempered by the fire of resilience. She had learned to love her flaws, to embrace her imperfections, understanding that her worth was not tied to her ability to conform but to her courage to be true to herself.

The newfound freedom she now felt was not just about outward expression; it was a deep, profound sense of liberation that emanated from the very core of her being. It was the freedom to choose her own path, to define her own happiness, to embrace her sexuality without shame or guilt. It was the freedom to love herself, flaws and all, to nurture her spirit, and to nourish her dreams.

The world stretched out before her, no longer a daunting obstacle course but a vibrant tapestry of possibilities. Each day felt like an adventure, an opportunity to explore her passions, to connect with others on a deeper level, and to express herself with authenticity. She had learned to trust her intuition, to listen to the whispers of her heart, and to follow the path that resonated with her soul.

The liberation she had found was not just about her own personal journey, but about the ripple effect it had on others. Her story became a beacon of hope, a testament to the transformative power of self-discovery. She used her voice to challenge harmful societal norms, to empower others to embrace their own freedom, and to create a world where everyone could live authentically and without fear.

Her journey had taught her that freedom is a continuous process, a constant evolution of self-discovery. It was a journey that never truly ends, but one she embraced with unwavering courage and a heart overflowing with love for herself and the world around her. She knew that the path ahead would still hold its challenges, but she was no longer afraid. She had found her own unbound soul, and with it, the unwavering belief that she could navigate life's complexities with grace, resilience, and a deep sense of self-love.

Inspiring Others

Amelia's transformation wasn't just about her own liberation; it was about creating a ripple effect that reached far beyond her own life. As she found her voice and embraced her authentic self, she inadvertently became a beacon of hope for others who were struggling to break free from the constraints of societal expectations and limiting beliefs. Her story resonated with women of all ages and backgrounds, who saw themselves reflected in her struggles and celebrated her triumphs.

Amelia's journey was a testament to the power of vulnerability and the transformative potential of sharing one's story. She became a voice for those who had been silenced, a catalyst for change, and an inspiration for countless others to embark on their own journeys of self- discovery. Her willingness to confront her fears, embrace her desires, and step outside of her comfort zone empowered others to do the same.

The impact of Amelia's story was felt in the lives of countless women who had been conditioned to believe that their worth was tied to their ability to conform to societal expectations. Her example challenged the notion that women had to choose between being "good girls" and "bad girls," demonstrating that they could embrace their multifaceted identities and find freedom in their own terms. Her journey served as a reminder that true liberation came from embracing one's authentic self, regardless of societal judgments or expectations.

One of the most powerful aspects of Amelia's story was her unwavering belief in the transformative power of connection. She found strength and support in the community she built, and she recognized the importance of sharing her experiences to empower others. Her story served as a reminder that we are not alone in our struggles, and that by sharing our stories and connecting with others, we can create a ripple effect of change and support.

Amelia's journey transcended the confines of her own life, leaving an enduring legacy that inspired countless others to embrace their own freedom and self-discovery. She became a symbol of female empowerment, a testament to the resilience of the human spirit, and a reminder that true liberation comes from embracing one's authentic self, regardless of societal expectations or limiting beliefs. Her story continued to resonate with generations to come, serving as a guidepost for those seeking to break free from the cages of societal expectations and live a life that is true to their own hearts and souls.

Creating Change

Amelia's journey of self-discovery didn't end with the liberation of her own soul. The freedom she'd found within herself, the power she'd claimed, and the strength she'd cultivated were not meant to be kept to herself. She realized that her journey was a ripple effect, a catalyst for change, a spark igniting the flames of self-acceptance and empowerment in others.

Amelia used her platform, a blog she'd started to document her experiences, as a voice for the unheard, a space for sharing stories and sparking conversations. Her words resonated with a vast audience of women, men, and non- binary individuals yearning for a world where authenticity and self-expression were celebrated, not condemned. She challenged harmful stereotypes about female sexuality, dismantling the notion that a woman's worth was tied to her adherence to traditional roles or the expectations of societal norms. She advocated for body positivity, encouraging acceptance of diverse shapes, sizes, and abilities. Her words became a powerful tool, dismantling the walls of shame and fear that imprisoned individuals in the cage of conformity.

Through her writing, she became a champion for marginalized communities, exposing the systemic injustices and inequalities that fueled societal prejudice and discrimination. She used her voice to raise awareness about issues like LGBTQ+ rights, racial injustice, and gender- based violence, encouraging her readers to become active participants in creating a more just and equitable world. Her platform became a haven for open dialogue, a space where difficult conversations could be had with empathy and understanding, fostering a sense of solidarity and collective action.

Amelia's activism extended beyond the digital world. She actively participated in local community initiatives, supporting shelters for women facing domestic violence, organizing fundraising events for LGBTQ+ organizations, and volunteering at schools to educate young people about healthy relationships and self-love. She used her newfound platform to amplify the voices of others, giving space to those who had been silenced and marginalized. She became

a mentor for young women struggling with body image, self-esteem, and societal pressures, offering guidance and support as they embarked on their own journeys of self-discovery.

Amelia's life became a testament to the power of vulnerability, a testament to the profound impact that one person's journey of self-discovery could have on the world around them. She demonstrated that true liberation wasn't just about personal transformation, but about using one's voice and influence to create a ripple effect of change, a wave of empowerment that reached far beyond her own individual experience. Her story became an inspiration for countless others, reminding them that they, too, had the power to break free from societal expectations, to embrace their authentic selves, and to become agents of change in the world. Amelia's journey was a testament to the indomitable spirit of humanity, a reminder that even in the face of adversity, we can choose to rise above, to break free, and to create a world where every soul is unbound and empowered.

Building a Legacy

Amelia's story, once whispered in the hushed corners of her own heart, now echoed through the halls of countless lives. It resonated with a symphony of voices, each carrying a unique melody of resilience, liberation, and the audacity to reclaim one's own narrative. Her journey, painstakingly crafted through years of internal battles and external challenges, had become a testament to the enduring power of self-discovery. The shackles of societal expectations, once firmly clamped upon her soul, had been shattered, leaving behind a woman who shone with the unyielding light of her authentic self.

Amelia's legacy wasn't confined to the pages of her own story. It extended outwards, touching the lives of those who dared to glimpse her courage. Her words, imbued with vulnerability and strength, found their way into the hearts of women who had long felt stifled by the rigid confines of societal norms. She became a beacon, illuminating the path to self-acceptance for countless individuals who, like her, had been taught to dim their own light.

Her story whispered to young girls, still grappling with the weight of expectations, that they were not destined to become mere reflections of the world's desires. It whispered to mothers, burdened by the weight of tradition and the relentless pressure to conform, that they held the power to carve their own path. It whispered to women of all ages, across cultures and backgrounds, that their worth was not dictated by the confines of social constructs but by the boundless potential that resided within their own hearts.

Amelia's legacy transcended geographical boundaries, extending across oceans and continents. It resonated in the bustling cities and quiet villages, reaching those who had long yearned to break free from the chains of conformity.

Her story served as a catalyst for change, a spark that ignited the flames of self-empowerment in the hearts of those who dared to dream of a life lived on their own terms.

Her words, etched upon the tapestry of time, became a guiding force for those seeking their own liberation. They whispered the truth of their inherent worth, urging them to embrace their vulnerabilities, to celebrate their imperfections, and to rise above the limitations imposed upon them by a world that often sought to diminish their brilliance.

Amelia's legacy was a testament to the enduring power of human spirit, a symphony of voices united by a shared desire for authenticity and freedom. It was a legacy that echoed through generations, ensuring that the whispers of self- discovery would continue to reverberate long after her story had been told.

The Power of Storytelling

Amelia's heart pounded in her chest, a drumbeat echoing the urgency of the truth she was finally ready to embrace. It wasn't just about her own journey, about the liberation she had fought so hard for. It was about the ripple effect, the way her story could resonate with others, sparking their own flames of self-discovery.

The whispers of doubt had been relentless, a chorus of voices echoing the fears she'd carried for so long. "Who are you to share this?" they murmured. "Your story is too personal, too raw. You'll be judged, ostracized." But the fire of her own truth burned brighter. She had wrestled with her demons, faced the darkness within, and emerged a woman transformed. Her story was a testament to the possibility of change, of breaking free from the shackles of societal expectations and embracing the wild, messy beauty of her true self.

She envisioned her words as a beacon of hope, a lighthouse in the storm for women struggling with similar internal battles. The pain, the fear, the struggle to find their voice— she understood it all too well. Through her writing, she could create a bridge, a connection, a space where vulnerability was celebrated, where silence was shattered, and where the shared experience of reclaiming one's power could blossom into a collective chorus of liberation.

The stories we tell ourselves, the stories society tells us, they have a profound impact on our lives. They shape our beliefs, our choices, and our very sense of self. For too long, Amelia had been bound by the narrative of the "good girl," a narrative that stifled her desires and denied her the right to explore the depths of her own being. Breaking free from that narrative, claiming her own story, had been a journey of immense personal growth. Now, she felt a responsibility to share that journey, to empower others to challenge the limiting narratives that held them captive.

She envisioned writing workshops and intimate gatherings where women could share their own stories, struggles, and triumphs. She envisioned books and articles that would spark conversations, dismantle harmful stereotypes, and challenge the status quo. The power of storytelling was undeniable. It had the power to heal, inspire, and ignite a revolution of self-acceptance and empowerment.

Amelia knew that her journey was far from over. There would be new challenges, new obstacles, and new lessons to learn. But she embraced the journey, the constant evolution, the ongoing process of self-discovery. And with each story she shared, with each voice she amplified, the ripple effect would continue to spread, creating a movement of women claiming their power, embracing their authenticity, and living lives that were truly their own.

The world needed their stories, the stories of women who defied expectations, who embraced their desires, who found their voice, and who dared to live a life that was unbound. Amelia's story was just the beginning, the catalyst for a collective awakening, a symphony of voices rising in unison, a chorus of liberation echoing through the ages.

The Journey Continues

Amelia's journey is not a destination, but a constant evolution. It's a tapestry woven with threads of joy, heartache, and everything in between. She understands that life is a series of chapters, not a single story with a neatly tied bow. Each new experience, each new relationship, each new challenge, is an opportunity to learn, to grow, and to redefine what it means to be truly free.

She's learned that freedom isn't about escaping the world, but about owning her place within it. It's about finding her voice and using it to speak her truth, even when it's uncomfortable, even when it challenges the status quo. She's learned that vulnerability is not weakness, but a source of strength, a way to connect with others on a deeper level and to build genuine, meaningful relationships.

Amelia knows that there will be setbacks, moments of doubt, and days when she feels like she's taking two steps back for every step forward. But she's also learned to trust the process, to embrace the journey, and to believe that even in the darkest of times, there is always light to be found.

She's surrounded by a community of women who are on their own journeys of self-discovery, women who understand the challenges of navigating a world that often tries to confine them. They are her sisters, her confidantes, her source of strength and inspiration. Together, they are a force for change, challenging societal expectations and creating a more inclusive and equitable world.

Amelia has learned to love herself unconditionally, embrace her imperfections, and celebrate the unique beauty that she brings to the world. She knows that her worth is not tied to her accomplishments, appearance, or ability to conform to societal standards. Her worth is inherent, reflecting her authentic self, the woman she was always meant to be.

She continues to explore, grow, and evolve. She's not afraid to challenge her own beliefs, step outside of her comfort zone, or embrace the unknown. She knows that the journey is never truly over, that there are always new adventures to be had, new experiences to be embraced, and new levels of freedom to be discovered.

And she wouldn't have it any other way. For Amelia, the journey is the reward, the constant process of self-discovery and self-actualization, a testament to the resilience of the human spirit, the unwavering power of the unbound soul.

Looking Back

The worn leather of the old armchair beneath me felt familiar, comforting. The scent of dust and forgotten memories hung in the air, a tangible reminder of the woman I was, the woman I had so desperately wanted to escape. I closed my eyes, letting the years unfold before me like a cinematic tapestry, each frame vivid and poignant.

It all started with that gnawing emptiness, a void that no amount of societal approval or religious devotion could fill. The perfect life, carefully constructed and meticulously curated, felt like a gilded cage. My 'good girl' persona, a shield against the world's scrutiny, was stifling, suffocating me with its own perfection. Then came the tremors, the cracks that appeared in the facade, the whispers of a yearning for something more, something wilder, and something undeniably me.

I remember the fear, the paralyzing terror of stepping out of the box, the imagined judgment of those who held me to their expectations. But the yearning for liberation, for self- expression, was stronger. It was an undeniable call, an irresistible siren song that beckoned me towards a path less traveled, a path that promised adventure and self-discovery.

The journey was a wild ride. Every step was a confrontation, a collision of my carefully cultivated self with the raw, unfiltered essence of who I was. I dove into the forbidden, exploring my sexuality, my desires, my vulnerabilities, all those aspects I had so carefully suppressed. There was shame, there was guilt, a whirlwind of emotions that threatened to pull me back to the safety of the cage.

But something shifted. I started to embrace the pleasure, the raw and untamed power that bloomed within me. I discovered a strength I didn't know I possessed: a voice that had been dormant for far too long. I learned to trust myself, to honor my intuition, and to stand up for my needs and desires.

The journey wasn't smooth. There were stumbles, falls, moments of doubt and despair. I confronted past trauma, the wounds that had shaped my perceptions of myself and the world. The healing was arduous, a slow and painstaking process of unpacking the layers of societal conditioning and societal expectations that had woven themselves into my very being.

And then came the realization. My worth was not tied to my ability to conform, to play the part of the 'good girl.' My value was inherent, an intrinsic truth that could not be defined by external standards. I learned to celebrate my imperfections, to embrace the flaws that made me uniquely me.

The journey was not just about self-discovery; it was about connection. I forged relationships with individuals who saw me, who celebrated my authenticity, who challenged me to grow and to embrace my power. They were my mirrors, reflecting back my strength and reminding me of my inherent worth.

The path to self-discovery is rarely linear. There were unexpected turns, setbacks that tested my resilience and threatened to pull me back to the safety of the familiar. But each obstacle, each challenge, only served to deepen my understanding of myself, to strengthen my resolve.

I confronted the ghosts of the past, the weight of familial expectations that had clung to me for so long. I learned to forgive myself, to forgive those who had hurt me, and to release the pain that had held me captive for so long. I set boundaries, prioritizing my own well-being, my own sense of autonomy.

Finally, I found peace with my roots, recognizing the influence of my upbringing while asserting my right to define my own path. I had become the architect of my own life, the author of my own story.

The woman I am now is a far cry from the woman I once was. I am a tapestry woven with the threads of my journey, a testament to the power of self-discovery, of self-love, of breaking free from the shackles of societal expectations.

I stand before the world, no longer a 'good girl' or a 'bad girl,' but a woman who has embraced the fullness of her being, the complexity of her desires, the beauty of her flaws. My soul is unbound, and it is a glorious, exhilarating feeling.

As I look back on my path, I see a tapestry of growth, a testament to the power of transformation. It is a journey that continues to unfold, a constant exploration of my depths, a never-ending dance of self-discovery.

The final chapter is not an end but a beginning. I am ready to embrace the future and face whatever comes my way with courage, resilience, and a profound sense of self-love. The unbound soul is a work in progress, a constant journey of self-discovery, a testament to the power of embracing the fullness of our being and the freedom that comes from living authentically.

Celebrating Her Freedom

The morning sun streamed through the window, casting a golden glow on the room. Amelia stretched, her body feeling lighter than it had in years. A feeling of pure liberation, a sense of untethered joy, danced within her. She stood, feeling the weightlessness in her limbs, a stark contrast to the heaviness she had carried for so long. This was freedom. This was the culmination of the arduous journey, unraveling the layers of conditioning and breaking free from the shackles of societal expectations.

She walked to the balcony, the crisp air filling her lungs, and gazed at the city sprawling below. The towering buildings, once symbols of ambition and the pressure to succeed, now felt like markers of a life she no longer desired. Her gaze settled on a woman walking her dog, who radiated an inner peace that Amelia craved for so long. It was a life of simple pleasures, of finding joy every day, of not being defined by achievements or accolades.

A wave of gratitude washed over her. This was her life now, a life she had fought for and created for herself. It was a life filled with the colors of self-expression, a symphony of her authentic desires, a tapestry woven with the threads of her design. She had embraced the power of her agency, refusing to be defined by the expectations of others. Her journey had taught her the power of vulnerability, the strength in embracing imperfections, the joy of speaking her truth, and the freedom to choose her own path.

Amelia took a deep breath, letting the scent of the morning air fill her senses. She had wrestled with demons, faced her fears, and emerged more vigorous, resilient, and liberated. She had learned to navigate the complexities of life with courage and grace, to find solace in her own company, and to celebrate the uniqueness that made her who she was.

Her reflection in the windowpane showed a woman beaming with newfound confidence, her eyes radiating the light of an unburdened soul. She had found her voice, reclaiming her power and using it to create a life that was truly her own.

The journey had not been easy, but it had been transformative. It had unlocked a wellspring of strength she never knew she possessed, which flowed with an unwavering belief in herself.

She no longer yearned for validation from the outside world. Her validation now came from within, from the unwavering belief in her own worth, the unwavering acceptance of her authentic self. She had embraced the 'bad girl' within, allowing her to dance with her desires, to explore the depths of her sensuality, to revel in the liberation of her own body.

Her past, once a source of pain and shame, had become a wellspring of wisdom and strength. She had learned to forgive herself and others, to embrace the imperfections that made her uniquely her. She had learned to let go of the past, to release the burdens of societal expectations, to step into the freedom of living authentically.

Amelia smiled, a smile that radiated with genuine joy. This was her life. This was her freedom. This was the unbound soul, dancing to the rhythm of its own heart, embracing the world with open arms, ready to meet the unknown with a sense of unwavering confidence, a confidence rooted in the unyielding power of her self-belief.

A Message of Hope

A Message of Hope

The Sun streamed through the window, painting the room in a golden glow. Amelia sat by the window, a steaming cup of tea in her hands. She had come so far. The journey had been tumultuous, filled with moments of exhilaration, crippling fear, and profound introspection. But she had emerged from the other side, a woman reborn.

She wasn't the same Amelia who had walked into the world with a carefully constructed persona, a facade of obedience and compliance. She had shattered the mold, the shackles of societal expectations, and the suffocating weight of conformity. She had finally met the "bad girl" who had lived within, hidden in the shadows for so long, and learned to embrace her wildness.

Now, as she looked back on her journey, she couldn't help but feel a surge of gratitude. She was grateful for the challenges, the heartbreaks, and the awakenings. They had all led her to this place of authenticity, freedom, and self-love. It was a place she had never dared to dream of, a place she had once believed was reserved for others, not for someone like her.

But here she was, a testament to the power of resilience, the strength of the human spirit, and the boundless capacity for change. She had broken free from the cage of expectations, the suffocating grip of societal norms, and the fear of her desires.

And now, she had a message for those still trapped, still grappling with the weight of their internal battles. "Don't be afraid to be you," she thought, her voice echoing softly in the quiet room. "Embrace your uniqueness, flaws, desires, and wildest dreams. Challenge the expectations, break free from the mold, and dare to live a life that is truly your own."

It wouldn't be easy, she knew from experience. There would be obstacles, moments of doubt, and voices whispering fear. But she also knew that the journey, however arduous, was worth it. The freedom she had found, the joy of living authentically, was a treasure beyond compare.

She thought of the countless women she had encountered on her own journey, women who had fought their own battles, challenged their own limitations, and found their own liberation. She saw their faces, struggles, and triumphs. She knew she wasn't alone and that others, too, could find the strength to break free.

"The expectations of others do not define you," she thought. "Your past does not define you, your fears, or your perceived limitations. You are powerful, beautiful, and resilient, capable of much more than you can imagine."

Amelia knew that the journey was not over and that there would be more challenges, lessons to learn, and layers to peel back. But she was ready. She was stronger now, more confident, and more grounded. She had learned to trust her own intuition, desires, and power.

She knew that as long as she held onto the truth of her own worth, as long as she continued to embrace her authentic self, she would find her way, even in the darkest of times. She would continue to break free, push boundaries, defy expectations, and live a life that was true to her heart. She would continue to be the unbound soul, a beacon of hope for others who yearned for the same freedom.

The Future is Unbound

The sun streamed through the window, casting warm squares of light onto the hardwood floor. Amelia sat at her desk, a cup of steaming tea warming her hands. Her eyes once filled with uncertainty, now held a quiet confidence. She had come so far, from the stifled girl trapped in a cage of expectations to the woman who finally set herself free.

This was not the end but the beginning. It was the start of a new chapter, a chapter where the possibilities were limitless. She had spent years yearning for something more: a life that resonated with her soul. She had chased that yearning, pushing herself to the edge of her comfort zone, exploring the depths of her desires, and confronting the shadows of her past.

The journey had been arduous, filled with challenges and moments of doubt. But with each hurdle she had overcome, with each step she had taken towards self-discovery, she had grown stronger and more resilient. She had learned to trust her intuition, embrace her imperfections, and find solace in her vulnerability.

She stood on the precipice of a future she had never imagined. The world stretched before her, a tapestry of possibilities waiting to be woven. She was no longer bound by the constraints of societal expectations or the limiting beliefs she had internalized. She was free to create her own story, to define her path, to live a life that was authentically hers.

Amelia had a newfound appreciation for the power of her agency. She had learned that freedom was not a destination but a constant journey, a commitment to living in alignment with her true self. It was about making choices that resonated with her soul, speaking her truth with conviction, and embracing life's messy, beautiful, and ever-evolving nature.

She was deeply grateful for the journey that had brought her to this point. The challenges had been transformative, the pain had been a catalyst for growth, and the lessons learned had shaped her into the woman she is today.

Amelia felt excitement as she gazed out the window at the vibrant world unfolding around her. There were adventures, dreams to be pursued, and a world to explore. She was ready to embrace it all, with a heart full of courage, a mind brimming with possibility, and a genuinely unbound spirit.

This was not just a new chapter in her story; it was a whole new book, filled with blank pages ready to be filled with her own unique experiences and vibrant colors. And she knew, with unwavering certainty, that she was ready to write it.

The End of the Story

The final pages of Amelia's story mark a culmination of her journey, a testament to her unwavering spirit, and a reflection of her transformation. Yet, this is not the end. It is merely a pause, a moment to breathe and to absorb the profound changes that have reshaped her very being. The journey of self-discovery is an ongoing odyssey, an endless exploration of the boundless depths of the human spirit.

As Amelia steps into this new chapter, the world around her feels vibrant, alive with infinite possibilities. Her senses are heightened, and every encounter and every experience is a potential catalyst for further growth. While still present, the echoes of her past no longer hold her captive. They are merely whispers of her evolution, reminders of the strength she has cultivated to navigate the complexities of life.

Amelia is now a beacon of self-expression, radiating authenticity and a newfound confidence. She has learned to embrace the contradictions within her, the 'good girl' and the 'bad girl,' recognizing that both are integral facets of her multifaceted identity. The boundaries that once confined her have crumbled, replaced by an unyielding determination to live a life true to her core values, a life that is a testament to the freedom she has claimed.

The world is a canvas, and Amelia is ready to paint with the colors of her creation. She is no longer bound by societal expectations and no longer seeks validation from external sources. Her validation comes from within, from the deep well of self-love and acceptance she has cultivated.

Her Journey has taught her that true freedom is not a destination but a way of being, a continuous process of becoming.

Amelia's story is not an isolated tale. It is a universal narrative that resonates with countless souls, a testament to the human spirit's capacity for transformation. Her journey reminds us that we all have the power to break free from the constraints of our past, challenge societal norms, and create a life that is authentically our own.

The ending of Amelia's story is the beginning of a new chapter, a chapter filled with uncharted territories and boundless possibilities. She is ready to explore, embrace, and continue to evolve, her soul forever unbound, her spirit forever free.

Acknowledgments

This book is a testament to the countless voices that have shaped my understanding of self-discovery and female empowerment. I am eternally grateful to the women who have shared their stories of resilience, vulnerability, and liberation, inspiring me to write this tale.

Thanks to every soul who provided support, feedback, or inspiration for their unwavering belief in this project. Your encouragement and insightful perspectives have been invaluable.

To my readers, I hope this story resonates with their journeys of self-exploration and encourages them to embrace their unbound souls.